COPSE 125

COPSE 125

A CHRONICLE
FROM THE TRENCH WARFARE
OF 1918

ERNST JÜNGER

author of
The Storm of Steel

★

HOWARD FERTIG

NEW YORK

First Paperback edition 2003
Published by Howard Fertig, Inc.
80 East 11th Street, New York, N.Y. 10003
All rights reserved.

Hardcover edition originally published
by Howard Fertig, Inc. in 1988

Library of Congress Cataloging-in-Publication Data
Jünger, Ernst, 1895-
    Copse 125.
    Translation of: Das Wäldchen 125.
    Reprint. Originally published: London : Chatto &
Windus, 1930.
    1. Jünger, Ernst, 1895-   . 2. World War, 1914-
1918—Personal narratives, German.   3. Germany.
Heer—Biography.   4. Soldiers—Germany—Biography.
I. Title.   II. Title: Copse one hundred twenty-five.
D640.J69613   1988   940.4′13′43   87-27174
ISBN 0-86527-445-2 (pbk.)

5 4 3 2 1

PREFACE

WHEN I joined up, the thought of all that lay hidden in the darkness of the future rejoiced me as indeed it did every other young fellow in those days. We knew already that an experience awaited us whose imprint on our development would be sharp and deep, and we saw in it a short and emphatic schooling from which, if we returned at all, we should return as men. We had seen the generation before us grow old in security, and it seemed a wonderful dream to be permitted to fight as soldiers for our country's greatness, ready to give all we had. We felt ourselves grow to meet the responsibility that suddenly rested all its weight upon our shoulders, and the past woke in us to make each a part of one terrific force. The word Fatherland like an old magic formula transformed us from the bottom, and loosing all ties of party and sect made us of one heart and mind. All of military age, to a man, thronged to the colours, eager to show by deeds that they were ready for the task their times laid upon them and that their country might rely upon them.

The spirit of those days will always betoken a culminating point and symbolize a supreme aim. It was stripped of all commonplace ; an ideal was its driving force. There alone is to be found the explanation of the miracles it achieved. There is no good asking ' What was the use of it all ? ' for we stood on the threshold of a realm that surpassed the limits within which a practical purpose can exist. Immortal deeds are absolute and stand from their outset in a realm apart. For a people they are an eternal fount of strength. We survivors will always be proud to have belonged to the youth of such a time.

In the course of the war we came next to recognize that its length as well as the unimagined violence of its phenomena made far more and quite other demands on our powers of endurance in body, soul, and spirit than we had foreseen. Months became years, and the pomp of battle a daily round of hard work. But at the same time the war, too, became a usual instead of an unusual state of affairs and dug itself permanently into us.

Those frightful landscapes were our daily surroundings where destruction ruled over all and nothing stood except the might of the soul that no force can subdue. In one thing alone we were great—in our aims that dwarfed the individual and made his life and fortunes of no account. Thousands died for an acre of ground, for a bit of trench, for a copse or a village—and rightly ; for the shaping of a world still hidden in the future was bound up with the gain or loss of scraps of ground like these. And the length of the war only heightened its intensity.

To stand thus, night and day without a breathing space, always on the alert ; to answer the great and utmost question of fate by the offer of one's own life—must not that be an education that goes deeper and lasts longer than any other ? And over and above it all to see the tangible success, the hoped-for and well-earned reward sunk in shipwreck utterly unforeseen—this is the severest trial that can be laid on a people, as on any single person who feels himself in heart and soul bound up with it. He who can pass a test like this shows that he is born for command and is fit for the exercise of power.

Certainly no one who is not carved out of the hardest wood goes on unshattered from such a schooling, and it is only in the day of distress that a nation can tell whether it has men at its disposal. We, too, have no lack of those who, like the Frenchman, Barbusse, regard war as a material affair and, turning its negative side outwards, endeavour to run up on the other a temple of peace and happiness. They give as their reasons devastated towns and frightful sufferings—as though our highest duty was the avoidance of pain. They have no mind to accept the responsibilities that demand sacrifice of such corruptible treasures as life and property when a nation's greatness and its ideas are at stake. It is here, though, that the greater moral strength lies, and there is no doubt on which side the materialists are to be found.

No—war is not a material matter. There are higher realities to which it is subject. When two civilized peoples confront one another, there is more in the scales than explosives and steel. All that either holds of any weight is in the balance. Values are tested in comparison with which the brutality of the means must—to any one who has the power to judge—appear insignificant. A strength of will, all-embracing and concentrated to the last pitch in the highest untamed expression of life asserting itself even in its own annihilation, is brought into play. The stake rises with the frightfulness of the battlefield on which it has to be upheld.

It was made plain to us that it was all or nothing. How could we have found the strength for an achievement whose meaning was not plain to us ?   Hence the war is more to us than a proud and gallant memory. It is a spiritual experience too ; and a realization of a strength of soul of which otherwise we should have had no knowledge.   It is the point of focus in our lives.   It decided our whole further development.   Whatever the fate that awaits us and whatever we may be called upon to do, we shall go forward in the rhythm of these decisive days, when our fate and that of Europe and, indeed, of the world were knit in one.   For even the bearing of the humblest soldier who fell somewhere in the night and the mist had a historical importance that will only gradually become clear.

I have twice already put on paper something of my own experiences of the war.   In writing this book I was inspired by the wish to select from them one episode and to use it as a means of presenting over and beyond the narrative of external events the sum of those forces and influences that clothed the men of our day as they faced each other in battle, and that by no means ended with the range of the guns.   I selected a comparatively quiet spell ; for a narrative in which active fighting played a leading part would soon lose itself in horrors.   And I selected a time at the close of the war when the race of trench soldiers—one of the hardiest and bravest that ever lived—was long since habituated to an existence that made the utmost possible demands, and was already inwardly and outwardly set in that mould that answers to a new age and its new methods.

Thus my choice fell on Copse 125,[1] one of the countless spots that for a few weeks were the central point of the lives and deaths of thousands of men—spots that once or twice perhaps were mentioned in a clause of the Army Report and are already utterly forgotten. It had not the least strategic importance, and yet at that time it had a meaning for all Europe as a local symbol of power where many lines of fate intersected, and against which were set in motion a strength in men and machinery that could have reclaimed a whole province. Hence it is well worth while to make it the point of a survey whose aim it is to reach beyond the episodal to the universal.

I had nothing to go upon but the page or two of concise notes in a diary—in part of merely personal interest—and these I have had to fill out from memory. But I have retained the diary form, for apart from letters it is the best for presenting every facet of a many-sided situation in a spontaneous manner. At the same time, in order to avoid endless repetitions, I have made some slight alterations in the order of events. In the course of the work it was borne in upon me that I was no longer in a position to separate after-the-war impressions sharply off from those of the war itself. I have made many observations that could not have been made in the form of a diary at the

---

[1] Known on English maps as Rossignol Wood. It is south of Arras and north of the Ancre, and is between one and two miles east of Hébuterne.—*Translator's Note.*

time. They are purposely dated back, since there is much the meaning of which has only now become clearer—and of this more than all, that the loss of the war, for the nation as well as for the individual, is only the destruction of a certain mould, but not of the essential reality, and that even during the war new ideas were already gathering force.

The actuality of power passes from one hand to another. Our turn too will come. Physical helplessness is a hopeless situation only when moral strength too has given out.   But it is just after a blow of fate that moral strength makes the most rapid growth.

COPSE 125

WHENEVER I begin to write again in this little notebook that fits so snugly into my map-case, the thought comes to me whether I shall ever write the last page of it. I have quite a pile of them at home by now, filled with orders of the day, brief observations and rapid sketches; and I look forward to happy times after the war, when I shall turn their pages and be able to remind myself how my days were occupied in these strange years.

Sometimes the writing is composed and careful and in ink; and I know at once that I was sitting then at my ease in one of those little cottages in Flanders or Northern France, or in a quiet sector in front of my dugout, smoking a pipe and disturbed at worst only by the distant hum of the last scout on his evening patrol of the sky. Then come disjointed and distorted lines in pencil, scrawled by the flicker of a candle in some overcrowded corner of a hellish hole before an attack, or during the endless hours of heavy shelling. Finally, sentences in agitated phrases, illegible, like the wave-lines of a seismograph recording an earthquake, with the ends of the words whipped out into long strokes by the rapidity of the writing—these must have been flung on paper after the attack, in shell-holes or fragments of trench swept by machine-gun bullets like a swarm of deadly hornets.

Yes, it would be jolly, in a quiet hour, such as one can hardly imagine now, to turn the pages of such memories with no care to weigh on one but how to spend the evening afterwards. It is for that alone now that I would care to live on. At home we are looked on as people who have so much courage that we don't care a fig for life. They know as little back there of the soul of the front-line soldier as they do of a monk's in Thibet. I have lived long enough in the trenches to know that there is not a man without fear, and if there were he would be no good ; for any one who is to be counted upon has a respect for his own existence and a deep sense of its absolute indispensability. It is no contradiction that we like to call each other condottieri and feel a strong affinity with those adventurous spirits who had so much blood in their veins that any pretext and any flag was a proper excuse for spilling it.

Men of this strong and courageous blood in which the superfluous vitality of a nation is shown, know well enough the value of life. They are more warmly and strongly alive to its joys than any others, and are well aware in the moment of battle of all that is at stake. But the balance of will and strength to the credit of a healthy race causes fear to retreat into the background as a dark shadow against which daring only shows up with a brighter fascination. Without fear there could be no courage, and a being who had no wish to live would be as little use in an attack as a machine.

I value no intercourse now, as far as the war is concerned, with any but its connoisseurs. Our experiences have separated us too far from ordinary life. If a year at the front counts for two in seniority, in the soul it counts for five at least. Immediately after the outbreak of the war, while it confronted us in all its unknown immensity and we saw only its surface-gleam of heroism, we could talk of it quite well and quite intelligibly ; but to-day, when we stand in the midst of it, we have got to know it from ever new and more puzzling sides.

I do not mean to suggest that this experience is the same for all. It differs, of course, completely according to personal capacity and temperament. One man has a mind for adventure and is thrown like a modern Sindbad from one danger to another. Another sees only the sanguinary glare on the face of events and is petrified as by the sight of a Gorgon's head. Another goes with the stream because he feels that fate is stronger than he is. He takes his quarters as they come ; trusts to his star in battle ; and even in the drear monotony finds his little pleasures growing like the bright lichens on a bare stone. Others again are soldiers first and last. Their eyes are hard and cold beneath the rim of the helmet. They are centres of energy about whom the wavering lines rally in the battle. In them the will-power of a nation at war seems to be most clearly and terribly expressed. For in the course of the last four years a type of fighting man has been evolved such as before could never have been dreamt of. At first, while it was a war of movement and all within and without was on a lavish scale, this contrast with earlier days was not observable. It arose when the spirit of the machine took possession even of the battlefields of Europe, and the flying man and the man in the tank and the scientifically trained leader of the storm-troop appeared. Then a thundering salute was fired to a new age and a new race of men ; blood flowed in streams and a hundred towns went up in smoke.

Nevertheless, in spite of all these differences between man and man, one feels how the great wave of this war heaves and sinks in one measure beneath every single one of us. Every society has its own development and each individual member partakes of it, though he may try by the oddest jumps and doublings to escape it. So, too, it is in the army.

And now, at this very moment, we seem to have entered upon a new and remarkable phase of the war. The mighty battles of the spring in which mechanical warfare reached an acme that can hardly be excelled, lie behind us. They have not brought the war to an end. On the heels of these exertions has come an inward weariness—in striking contrast to the huge masses of material whose employment has been brought to a standstill. One hears of symptoms of deterioration in the staff and in units coming from home or from the Eastern front ; and that surprises no one who knows from his own experience the interdependence of morale with health and bodily energy and the prospect of a victorious issue.

Here in the regiment, composed almost throughout of young men of a breed which in its impassivity seems to have been made for the war of material, this symptom takes another form. They will fight on with their old reliability from sheer sense of duty, but without expecting—I might almost say, without hoping anything. Routine comes markedly to the front. Boredom can be observed in their words and bearing. It extends even to their way of dying. A group of old trench soldiers with their heads together in a sunny corner of a traverse are talking in jerky phrases in which the common experience of years past is summed up ; and the spirit that binds them together is something of which no one in years to come will be able to form any idea.

Such are my surroundings. We moved up into the line to-night and it seems, making all allowance for our very modest expectations, to be a very quiet front. Perhaps the God of Battles will vouchsafe us a comparatively undisturbed abode for the summer.

The day before yesterday I still felt quite at home in the life of great cities Now I am housed once more in a fox's earth, with a foot of soil over my head. When I came back yesterday from leave I found the battalion in one of those God-forsaken hamlets in Northern France that have been derelict for four years and whose names for four years have followed us wherever we go, whether it be that we have to live in them or fight for their possession. Never on any bit of the world has so much blood flowed as between Arras, Bapaume, and Cambrai. Needless to say the battalion was already in marching order once more. Within two hours I had reported, taken over the company and turned out. When I felt the old comfortable army-coat about me, patched a hundred times in spite of its leather binding, I had already half forgotten my home—sickness for the fabulous land of beds with white sheets. My kit, too, was soon in order, for my present batman, August Schüddekopf, a trusty and unloquacious fellow from the Lüneburger Heath, whom fate spares me longer than it has his predecessors, has all my habits at his fingers' ends. He knows what goes in my haversack and what can be left for the ration party to bring up the line the next day; he puts my revolver, helmet, stick, and gas-mask ready to my hand, and finally asks the single question: ' What books are to go this time ? ' For if trench warfare is the most wearisome and laborious kind of fighting, at least it allows one a few luxuries in one's kit.

I am very pleased with him. His predecessor was a voluble fellow who had been a waiter. He very nearly brought me to despair, and when I wanted something to eat, he was capable of reeling off a whole menu though he knew well that there was nothing but bread and jam. It needs much mutual tact to live together without friction in the narrow confines of a dugout. The continual presence of an uncongenial person can become quite intolerable even when not a word is exchanged.

As soon as it was getting dark up came the lorries, and after the men had been parcelled out and stowed away like herrings, I got in beside the driver of the last one and off we went with short intervals between.

' Well, now for the big noises again,' I thought when the lorry started. At bottom, however, I was quite content, for though I have never had great cares I have never had so care-free a life as at the front. Every-thing is clear and simple. My rights and duties are prescribed. I need earn no money. My food is pro-vided me, and if things go badly with me I have a thousand fellow-sufferers, and above all, the shadow of death reduces every problem to a pleasant insignifi-cance. And though I had cancer or consumption I should not particularly care. The atmosphere is a manly and reckless one. All is staked on the throw, since, after all, one has marrow in one's bones and blood in one's veins. The ultima ratio of our guns is unanswerable. When these throats exchange their smashing, iron greeting, no further explanation is needed. Every one knows at once all about it. Here one can recover from the nausea of lies and etiquette and the feeble arguments of modern literature. The language of the guns is honourable and their arguments strike home. The expression ' steel bath of the war ' is good, too, although the journalists who have run it to death for years seem by degrees to be changing their minds. What are we to say about it ? Anyway it is a strong medicine—too strong for any but iron nerves. Only he who feels in himself the strength to conquer this dragon can be tempered in its hot blood. At worst it will be seen what is weak enough to be swept aside— and that in any case is of some value. We front-line soldiers, anyway, will certainly always hold our heads up and show that we cannot be put to the blush. It must be wretched to have one's fate fall in a great age without feeling oneself to be its child and its match, and without undergoing its influence as something new and never known before.

It is a wonderful June night. The sky is black and pricked out with a thousand stars. We drive of course without lights, but we need none, for the dusty road shows up clearly against the open field. The rifles and helmets clink together in the lorries. The engines sing the wild song of energy and tune our nerves more sharply than any march to a measure that seems to have drummed itself without his knowing it into the activities of the modern man.　Their song is something like this :

' Never did man go to battle as you do, on strange machines like birds of steel, behind walls of fire and clouds of deadly gas.　The earth has borne Saurians and frightful monsters.　Yet no being was ever more dangerously, more terribly armed than you.　No troop of horse and no Vikings' ship was ever on so bold a journey.　The earth yawns before your assault.　Fire, poison, and iron monsters go in front of you.　Forward, forward, pitiless and fearless !　The possession of the world is on the throw !

And as an accompaniment to this song of compression and explosion the ruins of farms and villages fly by on either side, waste-heaps of white chalk, torn and eviscerated by the pitiless talons of war.　The moonlight lies steelly and still as on an enchanted garden of evil, and the untended bushes of the waste gardens stand up as ghostily as in great cemeteries, motionless, and stirred by no breath of air.　A thick and heavy scent of corpses hangs over this landscape of death. Everywhere among the fields and at the entrances of the villages little crosses are stuck in the ground, and the shallow mounds in front of them are covered with shot helmets, smashed rifles, and rags of uniform.　This landscape we rattle through is well known to us all, and few of us have not a friend lying there whom we saw a few weeks ago during the great offensive and who now is left lying for ever.

And now we are already in the forward area, whose network of forces lies over the country like a web. We have to halt so as not to betray ourselves.　An

aviator, unseen in the far darkness of the sky, is drop-
ping parachute rockets that sway like a firework of sheet-
lightning over the road The searchlights' trembling
arms explore the dark vault.   At last one fastens on the
intruder and spits him like a small bright dragon-fly on
its white shaft of light.   Now the rest converge like the
tentacles of a sea monster and put him to flight.   Anti-
aircraft guns attempt to get him in the angle of their
fire, and one sees from the changing position of the
shrapnel bursts with what lightning speed the battery
commander gives his corrections.   Light-rockets are
discharged one after another, and even machine-guns
send out swarms of deadly glow-worms, in the hope
that even one may hit a vital spot in this costly unity of
man and machine and bring it down in flames or torn
to fragments.   One single bullet, six millimetres in size
and filled with blazing phosphorus—ah, if it could only
reach its mark to tell you : ' We have the best field-
glasses made by Zeiss, the best range-finders, and the
best machine-gunners.   Don't you dare come too near
us ! '   But the aeroplane, dancing like a pretty butterfly
among flame-flowers, makes a sudden bank that throws
it almost vertically on one wing and disappears in the
darkness of space.   We can proceed on our way.

The road gets worse.   Beside it lie smashed waggons,
carcases of horses strewn with lime, great heaps of
empty ammunition-baskets and shattered gun-carriages.
Sometimes we wind between deep shell-holes or over
heaps of masonry on the road.   Everything lies at
random, with the air of being left to its fate, for in this
region no work is carried out that is not strictly necessary.   The trees stand up bare with broken trunks or

stripped of their branches. Once we pass one of the giant heavy guns that lie hidden and silent : for they are reserved for critical hours. It is like a dangerous beast concealed in its lair of faggots and many-coloured patchwork ; only the mighty barrel rises steep and threatening in the air. To mask it, it is painted in irregular patterns, and all around an artificial wood has been planted.

Finally the lorries come to a stop. We have come within the zone of the field artillery, where as few targets as possible must be given and where the roads for wheeled traffic cease. Guides are waiting at a high embankment, in which the resting troops of this sector have their dugouts. The men get out and throw away their cigarettes ; and strung out in a long chain the march through the wilderness begins.

Our way lies over undulating country, grown over with long thin grass. In places the earth is thrown up and churned by shells—as recently as yesterday or to-day, by the look of them. I walk beside one of the guides—an old soldier, as I recognize not of course from his iron cross, but from the ring of his voice, and from a certain superiority that comes out in the remarks he lets fall—short and to the point. I think I shall be able after the war to pick out these fellows, or the members of the younger generation who have the same stuff in them, infallibly from a crowd of any size, though doubtless it is just they who will say least when the war is mentioned. In the course of years a feeling of kinship and solidarity has grown up that is almost unmistakable.

He tells me that this part of the line is not too grand

—dugouts bad, trenches fallen in, enemy patrols very active, and heavy losses within short periods. For the moment my impression is not so bad as that. The sheet-lightning of the guns on the horizon is not much to speak of, and the Verey lights go up at sober intervals. Further to the right there seems to be a rather sore spot. Heavy stuff bursts over it without ceasing. The shells follow each other so closely that the ear can scarcely distinguish one from another, and a fiery glow burns in the sky. Far away to the left, too, where the front makes such a bend that it seems to be almost at our backs, it must be properly ' windy.' Perhaps the Army Report, the greatest and most laconic journal in the world, will allude once more to heavy shelling on some parts of the front—a phenomenon of which no one can form any conception who has not been present at it.

Nevertheless I press on hurriedly. A march through unknown country always affects the nerves. Sudden bursts of shelling may come along. Then one loses the guide and wanders about all night and finally, perhaps, as has happened thousands of times, walks straight into the enemy lines. The savage landscape, too, turns one's fancy inevitably to a whole succession of imaginary alarms that the brain is incessantly at work to dispel —and this, when it goes on and on, is more exhausting than one thinks.

For this reason we are glad to reach the outskirts of an utterly dilapidated village that lies, we are told, just behind the front line. A narrow trodden path winds through what were once farmyards, gardens, and hedges. Here the optical delusions just alluded to are of course particularly vivid. The feelings are not easily reconciled to the chaotic and meaningless. They endeavour to complete and to construct and to fill empty spaces with strange phenomena. Shimmering palaces and clear regular structures rise up, or dark low buildings emerge that lurk in the desolation like taverns of ill repute or ruined mills. Their outlines run and boil up, die away, or change into one another; probably it is the pale moonlight that originates this diaphanous architectural music which accompanies one's thoughts and torments them. Something unspeakably tragic and ghostly emanates from the deserted homesteads ; an infinite sorrow lingers among the ruins.

In front of the village an immense crater-field extends, shell-hole on shell-hole. We vanish into a low and often discontinuous communication trench. A few parties of the troops we are relieving meet us. Hastily, without exhanging a word, we press past them. The trench system is a close and complex one. Here and there the entrances to dugouts are sunk in the walls. We cross a strong, well-built trench, where the posts stand motionless. This is the main support line. Now we have the front line before us and then we have reached our goal.

But what 's this ? We have counted our chickens before they are hatched ; and till now it all went smoothly. I find myself crouching next the guide in a corner of the trench without knowing quite how I got there. And here it comes again ! A volley of shrapnel whose pressure on the air makes a screaming sound as it rends its way through it ; then blinding flashes of flame close above the ground, explosions, whistling

swarms of bullets and pattering smacks on the soil—
all in one moment.   A smell of burning, vaporous and
smarting, drifts along the trench.   Behind us—an outcry
and curses ; a figure in full equipment stumbles over
me, picks himself up and runs on.   Schüddekopf
emerges out of the darkness and pulls off my helmet.
Once more I seem to have got away with it.   As I go
on I take a look at the corner where we took cover and
see that in this fraction of a second we found time to
hit upon the safest spot and to make use of it.

We are now only a few steps from our goal.   My
escort stops before a burrow hung with ragged and
splinter-torn canvas.   A little signboard—' Company
Commander '—is nailed to the outer framework, and a
gleam of light shows through.

' Hallo ! '

' What 's up—the relief ? '

' Relief ! '

At once all is astir below.   I make my way down.
Schüddekopf and my orderly leave their packs outside
and follow.

Down below we find the usual scene—the minute
table, with boxes of bombs as chairs, the stove, and
three beds of wire mesh, built lengthways into the wall.
A bayonet is stuck into the wall between two of the
casing boards and on its handle a candle flickers.   A
Verey-light pistol and a bunch of bombs hang from a
wire.   The telephone is in one corner, to be used in
emergency only.   It is insulated against enemy listening apparatus.   This is one of the holes in which for
years the youth of whole nations has been at home, one

of those confined and noisome forts which so often have been tombs.

My predecessor, a colour-sergeant, is seated at the table, with his belt buckled, his helmet on his head, ready to be off. After a brief greeting I sit down beside him to take over ; for I know that after a long spell in the line one is glad to turn one's back on the trenches as soon as possible. I am given a memorandum concerning the sector, the air-photographs, and the trench-map, while the orderlies check the reserves of ammunition.

After a few more particulars have been mentioned, the three runners from the platoons come in and hand over small chits on which it is stated that their respective posts have been taken over. To one of them is added the report that two men were slightly wounded during the relief. So the little burst of shelling did not pass quite without losses. Now we too can write out a similar chit which, signed by both, is sent back to the battalion commander. Now we have done. My predecessor wishes me a quiet time and takes his departure. He comes down again, though, to tell me of a block in a sap running out from the front line. I know this intimate feeling for a sector well. In spite of all, one loves it, because of all the labour spent on it and all the reflections on its eventualities. It becomes as familiar almost as a living being. Earlier, in the heyday of trench warfare, when we still lived in strong trenches and dug ourselves into them for months together, and equipped them with reinforced concrete and underground communication trenches, that intimate feeling was stronger than ever.

At last I am alone.   I light a cigarette and go out to
have another look at the night.   The moon has set.
Damp and silent lies the stretch of land for which my
mere signature has made me responsible, this bit of
land a thousand metres long and five hundred deep,
with its system of excavations and communications, in
which lurk a hundred and fifty armed men and over
whose front the pressure of a finger can draw a curtain
of flame.

This bit of land that any moment may turn into a
crater of flame is the holding we are now to farm and
where we ourselves perhaps will be the seed-corn.
Behind us away to the east lies the land whose will to
live is embodied in our willingness to die, and before
us, invested with flame, there where the muzzles of our
guns are pointing, lies the enemy.   Between these two
mighty forces runs No-man's-land, watched by countless eyes like the index of a scale.

All is quiet.   To the front a Verey light glides now
and then snake-like into the sky—that is the officer on
trench duty making himself acquainted with the lie of
the land.   I can lie down for an hour or two ; for there
is a man posted just by the dugout who will give the
alarm at the first sign of any disturbance.   To make
sure I ask him once again the signal for the barrage and
counter-barrage, as well as for a gas-attack, and then
go down again into the dugout, where Schüddekopf in
the meanwhile has made things a bit more comfortable,
and lying down, pull the blanket over my head.

THE first morning has been spent in getting to know the trench well enough to find my way about in it by day or night, rain or shell-fire, without a moment's thought.

The sector is designated by the letter A. It forms, therefore, the right flank of the regimental front. Before it the ground rises slightly to an extensively wooded country, and in between can be dimly seen the light brown soil thrown up from the English trenches. On the right it is linked up with the next regiment by an unoccupied length of trench. On the left it joins with the next company's sector. I have visited the officers in command on each flank.

A number of broad half-fallen-in communication trenches lead back to the main support line, and behind again, separated from us by undulating ground, is the village we passed through last night. Its name is Puisieux-au-Mont, or, as we should say, if I am not mistaken, Bergbronn. We can only see the higher parts of it—a few isolated heaps of masonry and the ruins of the church surrounded by the stumps of trees, a great reddish-brown stone-heap, which the English apparently suspect to be an artillery observation-post ; for during almost the whole morning it was visited with heavy flat-trajectory shells that screamed on their way high over our heads.

The trenches are extremely ruinous, washed in by the rain, low and wide. In some places an attempt

has been made to prevent them from being entirely
flattened out by shoring them up with timber. They
form part of the old strong trench system fought over
during the Somme battle, and then evacuated by us
when we had blown up all the dugouts ; and at last,
after lying derelict for a long while, retaken again in the
March offensive. It is a neighbourhood, then, that has
already seen much ; and this explains why there is
scarcely a spot that is not turned up by shell-holes.
Most of them certainly have been healed over by a
thick matting of grass, but this is already being torn
again by countless fresh wounds.

A trench system, then, was there ready for us, but it
has the unpleasant feature of being directly connected
with the enemy's lines by a number of saps. These
saps are, needless to say, blocked with concertinas and
knife-rests of barbed wire and guarded by outposts
and machine-guns. But nevertheless they are the
starting-points for every enemy patrol. Another
peculiarity of this front is that it has not a trace of wire
entanglements in front of it. That speaks well for our
attacking spirit, but all the same this discovery gave me
a very unpleasant feeling. The three seconds before
an attacking party can get over the wire, and during
which it has to expose itself to full view, puts such long
odds on the defence that they should never on any
account be forgone.

Little can be said for the dugouts either. They are
what are called Siegfried dugouts, that is to say, semicircular holes, penetrating the wall of the trench to a
distance of three metres and protected from above with
a covering of earth, at the most two metres deep. The

frame consists of thin circular sheets of corrugated iron
that scarcely support the weight of the earth heaped
on them and give only just room enough for two men
to lie at length.   In any case the men who make
them are better off than those who bivouac in them
and who in their moments of rest keep their eyes
fixed on the zinc roof, the mouse-trap that must infallibly crush them at the first direct hit.   Dohmeyer,
whom I found reposing in one of them after trench duty,
beside his batman, when I paid my visit to the sector
on my left, showed his optimism in finding the one com-
forting remark to be made upon them: ' If these things
weren't springy,' he said, ' then it would be rotten.'

The only cover in the whole of our front that could
with any decency be called a dugout is in my occupation.   That alone—apart from its inappropriate situation behind the right flank of the neighbouring sector—
would be a conclusive reason for exchanging it for
another as soon as possible.

Compared with earlier days, then, when we dug
ourselves ten metres and more into the earth, there has
been a serious decline in security.   What strongholds
we used to have, with galleries as long and comfortable as a Dickens' novel, whence left and right
there opened out living-rooms and sleeping-rooms and
ammunition-chambers and exits and entrances and
cross-communications, and where one could traverse
one's whole front like a mole without once coming to
the surface.   At Monchy, besides a comfortable dugout
for quiet times, where a wide shaft directed the light
of day straight on to my writing table, I was master of
an underground dwelling approached by forty steps

hewn in the solid chalk, so that even the heaviest shells at this depth made no more than a pleasant rumble when we sat there over interminable games of cards. In one wall I had had a bed hewn out, immense as the box-beds of Westphalian cottages, where, protected from the slightest noise and encased in stout oaken boards, I slept in a casket of soft dry chalk. At its head hung an electric light so that I could read in comfort till I was sleepy. The walls were adorned with pictures in colour from *Jugend*, and the whole was shut off from the outer world by a dark-red curtain with rod and rings ; it was displayed to visitors, with a running commentary of jest, as the last word in luxurious depravity. In those days, secured by wire fifty metres wide, one could venture to sleep in pyjamas, and the automatic that lay to hand beside the ash-tray was only used when it was desired to break the monotony by going on patrol. Those were splendid days.

But now. . . . The war has become more mobile and such works of construction no longer pay. And then it must be admitted that with the attack on Verdun the series of great onslaughts of material made the contrast between the safety of these gigantic strongholds and the front-line trenches, swept with flame and shattered with shell, far too great. But apart even from the moral factor, the occupants of these caverns, in the event of an attack, had as far to go before they could reach the trench as if they had to climb the stairs of a four-storeyed house. Thus it often happened that they had a warm reception half-way up from bombs and burning phosphorus without being able to strike a blow, particularly when the men on guard in the trench had long since given their lives in its defence without any one below being any the wiser.

Hence, after a particularly tragic disaster on Vimy Ridge, an order appeared one day that no dugout in the front line was to be more than two metres deep, and that all those already in existence were to be blown up.

What this iron order meant can be understood only by those who know the mass of stuff that, often without a break for weeks together, was flung on the trenches.   To have to crouch under fire without cover, belaboured without a pause by shells of a calibre sufficient each one to lay a fair-sized village in ruins, without any distraction beyond counting the hits mechanically in a half-dazed condition, is an experience that almost passes the limits of human endurance. For this reason the men who issued the order, and threw hundreds of thousands naked and defenceless into the fire, took on themselves one of the heaviest responsibilities the mind can conceive.   And yet, even though I may be one of the victims, I can but admit they were right.   Time works with heavy tools, and in the battle for some slag-heap of horror, over whose wreathed smoke rival conceptions of the world's future are locked in demoniac strife, it is not a question of the few thousand men who may perhaps be rescued from destruction, but of the dozen or two survivors who are there in the nick of time to turn the scales with their machine-guns or their bombs.   That is a view of the world's destiny which few have the iron nerve and masculine force to bear, and yet one may be proud to live in a time when such a spirt has shaped events to its mould of tempered steel.   Though few may emerge from these flaming plains that offer no shelter but the mettle in a man's own heart, and though these few, resolute in aim and act, may still find fate turn against them and deny them their goal, yet I feel as surely as I feel anything at all that a gain will be scored that can never be scored out. For they who can come through this—and, as I say, there can only be a few—what can there be that they could not come through ? And so I see in old Europe a new and commanding breed rising up, fearless and fabulous, unsparing of blood and sparing of pity, inured to suffering the worst and to inflicting it and ready to stake all to attain their ends—a race that builds machines and trusts to machines, to whom machines are not soulless iron, but engines of might which it controls with cold reason and hot blood. This puts a new face on the world.

However, to come back to our bit of the line and its defence, fraction though it be of the great task. When I got back to the dugout I studied the memoranda, written with an eye to brevity and in strict conformity with the latest conceptions of warfare. The warfare of position is not merely an experience in space in the course of which one has to be slaughtered without turning a hair, but a complete problem, ruled by the tactics uppermost at the moment and presupposing, as in chess, a knowledge at the least of the elementary facts and their possibilities. The conditions are made up of the terrain, which is always radically the same, of the constantly changing factor of weapons, of the strength of the two opponents, and of the quality of the fighting troops—which has always turned the scale and always will.

The backbone of the position is the main support line ; and this is to be held without fail. In front of it, clearly visible from every point, extends the forward zone—where the action to be taken depends on the strength of the attacking forces. In the event of minor attacks, the trenches are to be defended ; in the event of a major operation there is to be a retirement on the support line, after keeping the enemy under fire till the last possible moment. This is a precarious movement to carry out, as it entails getting through not only the enemy fire, but our own, which comes down in full force in front of the support line at the first signal, without distinction of friend or foe.

There is no disguising the truth that these measures are not the highest development of the elastic scheme of defence, which, first bending back before an enemy who is gradually losing impetus, rebounds again like a tightened cord of steel to hurl him back. In the first stages of trench fighting we knew nothing but the fixed line. It was contested to the last, and if it broke a new one appeared behind it. During the Somme battle these lines, in which the losses often amounted to a complete annihilation, were filled up again and again with men, until it was realized that it could not go on ; and then the plan was to split up the enemy fire by confronting it with a wide surface instead of one clearly recognizable line. That is where we are now, after experiences dearly paid for by heavy sacrifices. But what good is the zone to us when its useless extent is clearly marked by the outlines of two or three trenches ? It only means that the weight of fire is divided by three, a weight that since the Somme days has been multiplied by twenty.   And what is the state of affairs in a trench, which at the very moment of an attack is invaded by a mob of exhausted men who have taken to flight by order ?   Giving ground, as it is so beautifully expressed, does not come naturally to the German soldier, and he will never be able to get properly used to it. Further, all instructions that give the moral coward the least shadow of a pretext are bound in war to take a bitter revenge.   There is here no room for compromise. There is room for nothing but fighting to a finish.   All else is swept off the board.   For this reason phrases such as 'under circumstances,' 'given the case,' ' possibly,' should be found in no tactical treatise.

It will be proved to the hilt, if the war goes on, that whether in attack or defence, fighting can only be done in zones.   But we must at the same time manage to rid ourselves once and for all of the disastrous idea of the line with which history and the drill-yard have saddled us all through the war.   The simile of the steel cord, that I introduced just now, is equally false.   The right one is that of a net into which the enemy may certainly penetrate here and there, but where he will at once be overwhelmed from all sides by a web of fire.   Like the magician's apprentice, we have never made ourselves thoroughly masters of the weapons whose power we dispose of.   We do not realize that the frontal volley at short range is done with.   We fight now with long-range machinery, diminutive centres of energy radiating a deadly effectiveness.

We shall no longer hold our ground shoulder to shoulder, but isolated from one another in small groups and distributed far and wide over the smoking country, conductors of elemental forces. And in the same way we shall attack as an army in echelon composed of venturesome machinery, under cover of rings of fire and armoured aeroplanes, and controlled from a central point by flash-signals. Here we have the picture of the great battle of automata which consists in this—that two strongly organized and yet at all points highly mobile zones of power, whose molten edges flow into one another, attempt to turn each other from an ordered array into a chaos of useless iron and enervated mobs. A test like this, in which a number of entirely unpremeditated battles will necessarily be set in motion at one time, will give the clear and in-contestable proof whether a nation deserves to survive, or whether it has played its part and must make way for a stronger and therefore a better one. Its equip-ment will be put to the proof and weighed up, its achievements, therefore, in science and industry—in short, only the best and most fit will be in the running. Indisputable testimony will be given, in the discipline of large bodies of men and in the capacity of the command for bold organization on a large scale, of a nation's fitness for empire. And finally, it will be shown whether a civilized nation has so much future left it, and so compelling an appeal to its sons, that it can find hundreds of thousands of young men of high in-telligence and iron heart who have still life's joys before them and yet, in the midst of the frightful loneliness of battle, count the destruction of all they know and are and might be as nothing compared with the greatness of the idea within them. All this will come to the ordeal and much more besides. It is to be hoped that we shall always have a manhood to meet this test with joy and courage ; it is equally to be hoped that it may not fall to the lot of every generation.

We shall always be proud nevertheless that it fell to our lot.

WHEN I read what I wrote yesterday, I detect something almost of reproach against our command for having been slow to draw the tactical conclusions from the alteration in the effectiveness of weapons and for leaving the troops to fight in antiquated formation. Such is far from my intention even in these entirely personal notes and at a time when know-alls come up like mushrooms. Nothing could be more ghastly than a pedantic and sudden change of the straight battle-front. No one would know where he was and every invertebracy would find its tactical back-door. Already notions like that of ' giving ground before attacks of considerable weight ' cause disaster and confusion enough. A straight front, ruled firm and clear in the very flesh and blood, even when it does not quite answer to the situation of the moment, is better than a constant change of principles—that is the same in a soldier's education as in every other. It has to be remembered, too, that the conflict between two well-matched and well-equipped opponents takes its own form up to a certain point. For example, if we find it altogether too hot for us in the trench, we need no telling to take up positions in front and behind, and there we have our zone occupied in extension and depth.

This morning I moved into a dugout I discovered yesterday when I was wandering about in a maze of abandoned trenches behind the front line. It was soon done after I had sent Schüddekopf ahead to put it in order.

And now I am in possession of a real summer residence. It is an ancient burrow without steps or door, dating perhaps from the end of 1914, which seems to have been forgotten ever since. There is nothing inside but a half-mouldering bench of three narrow planks. On this I have put a mattress of grass, whose sour fermenting odour already fills the air. After Schüddekopf had swept out a few rusty jam tins, empty bottles, and bits of newspaper and a host of huge steel-blue caraboids with a leafy branch, I took possession of this Robinson Crusoe's hut, into which the sun shone through a curtain of bindweed and clover, and found myself very comfortable there. My modest resources helped to make much of the surroundings. Close to the entrance there is a deep recess broken away in the wall of the trench, and it only needs to be edged off in the right way to support a table and bench of dugout-boarding that could not be bettered for summer weather. Immediately behind the dugout a heavy shell has scooped out an immense crater to which I will dig a little approach, and there, undisturbed by the coming and going of despatch-runners, of which there will soon be plenty, bake myself in the sun.

This whole bit of trench will be squared up and deepened so as to avoid unnecessary head wounds and carried further to meet a communication trench near by, and then there will be thoroughfare to the front-line trenches. A few traverses away from me, Schüddekopf and Schmidt, the company runner, are building themselves a tin Siegfried, and close to them will be a machine-gun section, so that we shall be able, particularly as we are on higher ground, to make ourselves felt if it comes to a fight.

I once had an instructor in tactics who gave us the good advice to resolve every bit of country on our walks into its tactical elements. Lest I should approximate to this portentous ideal of the sheer man of purpose, I took the pains to-day to imbibe the landscape for its own sake, the same landscape that I traversed yesterday with the mental absorption of a man set on one aim only. The best opportunity for this was after I had put the men on trench work.

The rays of the morning sun are already hot on the treeless land. The fields over which the scythe has not passed for years are a mass of wild-flowers. They bathe the trenches in a hot stream of scent, made of a thousand aromatic and volatile essences, borne upon the acrid ground-swell of the grass shrivelling beneath the scorching sun. The swarms of insects are mad for joy—wrought up to the highest pitch of their vital energies. It is they who seem to be the meaning and the real content of the landscape. Clouds of crystalline wings and brightly coloured scales dance above the trenches, and their million-fold humming and chirping and buzzing drowses one like a great monotonous song that is forgotten at last in a dream. The air shimmers over colours as bright and glowing as the scum on molten lead, an enamel broken only by the dull earth-brown of the countless shell-holes. On the horizon the light glances on the ruins of Puisieux. Looking at the white roofless walls surrounded by the skeletons of trees, one might fancy oneself surprised by the ghostly apparition of a phantom and extinct oasis in the midst of a desert. Not a sign of life as far as the eye can see, and death itself seems to have fallen asleep ; for not a shot breaks the midday stillness of the front. No sound and no movement betrays the presence of whole regiments in hiding. There is utter peace, and only nature speaking to itself.

And yet the eye cannot lose sight of the mighty contest that cleaves a land made, one would think, only to be ploughed and reaped. The cleavage follows the boundary between Artois and Picardy, those two rich and ancient provinces whose population strangely mingles Gallic sensibility with Flemish calm. It is a fertile land of age-old history, a wide and smiling plain, rising at times in gentle undulations, well watered and thickly populated. I am a North German reared in a hard-favoured country, often shrouded in mist and covered with heather and peat moss, and the loveliness of this country, in the parts of it that the war has not reached, has often put me in the humour of an untroubled pastoral play. The parks of the innumerable country houses that still have a breath of the old régime about them, though perhaps for long enough a merchant or a Paris banker spends his summers there, are still in great part maintained as they were laid out, in the clear and formal style of Lenôtre ; the many little churches over which in those days Fénélon, banished from the court of the Roi Soleil, exercised his mild sway from his archiepiscopal throne at Cambrai, are still crowded every Sunday ; and the country towns, where life stagnates in drowsy comfort, still present the same sleepy exterior—though beneath its calm reflections the Balzacs and the Stendhals found passion as hot and intrigues as finely spun as everywhere else in the world.

Now, however, all that is erased like the delicate evanescence of pastel, and a stylus of steel has been drawn across the land from here to Flanders on one hand and to the Vosges on the other. Strong bulwarks traverse its fields and mighty guns stand in readiness in its devastated villages. The plains where now a rich harvest would be ripening to gold, wear a fixed and heroic mask whose hollow eyes make a lonely spectator tremble. Even if some one who knew nothing of all that has passed were suddenly to be set down here, the spirit of annihilation would creep into his heart, for its features are engraved in this earth and its chill seems to mingle its dark reflex with the very rays of the shimmering sun.

Let it not be thought that we look unmoved upon the desolation of this corner of sunny France into which we have been driven by forces stronger than ourselves. It would be utterly intolerable if we might not dream that new life surges up beneath the desolation. It must bear the fate it has not deserved, as we bear ours. It will not be spared, for nothing is spared when the future of nations is at stake. For any one of its quiet and obscure villages may be stormed to-day and known to-morrow in every portion of the globe. Each one may play a part in a chapter of history that disposes of provinces and empires. Hence, we must be as hard as stone. Fields will be tilled again and villages rebuilt and men multiplied beyond all need—but time and fate go by once and then no more.

THE work has gone on quicker than I expected and I am now finally installed, and the trenches have got me once again in their day-by-day spell. To our satisfaction we find that the artillery leaves us in comparative peace. We seem to be almost overlooked. The focus-point of our front is undoubtedly two company sectors further to the left, in Copse 125, where there must often be some thoroughly nasty business going on. To set against this, our communication trenches, particularly where they cross the village, are often under fire. There are several hollows, where presumably movement has been observed, which are very heavily shelled at certain hours of the morning and evening and, for the time, almost hidden beneath clouds of dust and vapour. Owing to this, besides the casualties during the first relief, we have had three more wounded, among them a sergeant—all on ration-parties. Worse is the outbreak of a severe form of influenza which is said to have come from the enemy's trenches. It puts its victims entirely out of action. Nearly every morning two or three men have to be sent back. They are feverish and crouch listlessly in their dugouts, and we shall not see them back again very quickly. If it goes on, we shall have to reduce the number of the posts—a serious measure, considering we are completely without wire.

The morale, in general, is as good as can be expected of troops so greatly exhausted. I hope the comparative quiet will have a good effect. Rations, too, ought to be improved without fail. These things are not in themselves the flame that soldiers rather pedantically call the moral factor, but they are the oil without which it cannot continue to burn. It has to be reckoned, too, that a body of soldiers does not naturally consist solely of heroes out of Ariosto, fine, perhaps, as that would be, but for the most part of men who are not used to exercising their reason beyond the limits of their daily bread. If they are left hungry they ' understand the world no more,' and may become very discontented indeed. And this discontent, with all the friction it sets up—to a degree that no one who has not experienced it can imagine—does not vent itself on those who are responsible for the rations (though they too would naturally rather see us fed with chunks of meat than potato meal), but on the head of him who crouches in the trenches with them and has little enough to laugh about without that.

So the other day, when we were out of the line, I felt compelled to clear up this endless grievance of the dinner hour once for all. I talked at length and told them exactly what each man's ration was—so many grammes of potatoes, so much bread, so much vegetables, so much meat, so much coffee-substitute, and so much ' portion.' And when I asked if it was all clear one of them answered : ' We don't doubt we get it, sir. But it 's too little—it does not fill us up.' What is one to say to that without being ridiculous ? For these fellows, simple as they seem, perhaps, have a damnably keen sense of the ridiculous, and any one who tries to come it over them with the old phrases current among the top-hats and leather helmets, finds he has come to the wrong address. They listen to him with the greatest composure, and when he has gone one of them only needs to say ' That was a nice chat ' and they all understand each other without further comment. In the surroundings in which these fellows have to do their duty all phrases are swept away, as all else that is superfluous, varnished and gummed on—-and you can't mistake it !

The power to influence men, of which nowadays there is so much talk that one feels that it must be in a bad way, is one of those qualities that can never be acquired even though a whole lifetime were spent in the study of it. Its root lies in the temperament, not in the will ; and in it speaks the race, not the individuality—valuable as this may be, too, in itself. Hence it is quite independent of speech. I have had section leaders, regular dry Lower Saxons who do not speak twenty words in the day, and yet they have their eight men under their control like one. That supreme type of leadership, too, the race-proud Prussian officer, who reached his highest development in 1866 and is still, thank God, not extinct, has never wasted words.

Of late they have been sending fellows among us who, under the title of education or instruction officers, give lectures to the men about our industry, our predominance as a world-power, our threatened interests in Eastern Asia, or the Bagdad railway—lectures whose merits are indisputable, but all that is far too remote to interest the great majority of the men. They go to the lectures, though they have quite enough without, as they would to any other duty or fatigue. It would be of no value, either, if they knew it all. They would be none the better for it. Wars are won—whatever one may say—by the heart, not by the brain ; by the enthusiasm that launches a host like one man—why they scarcely know, except that the deep consciousness of natural and utterly incontestable right possesses them. When the common soldier goes into battle in good form and good heart he does more for our interests in Eastern Asia or anywhere else than by knowing all about our historical and lawful pretensions. The pretensions of the other side may be even better grounded than ours. That is a matter of indifference. For it is not justification that turns the scale, but the stronger and more deeply realized will to power If it were not so, the blood-test of war would have no meaning. As for arguments, they can be thrashed out by the intellect alone and very much less expensively beforehand.

The matter is simpler and yet more difficult too. The man in the ranks feels that we are in the right and does not need to have it explained to him. Three months ago, when every night, week after week, the gigantic movements of men and material rolled westward to the final offensive, it was plain to all who and what we were, and what our right was to live and have dominion—much plainer than a thousand lectures could have made it. And then when, on 21st March, the single thunderclap of twenty thousand guns sought to convince the whole world of it, each one of us knew in his heart and with pride that one mighty will spoke in fire and explosive and steel. That is the feeling that wins battles. That is the soldiers' inspiration, marching, fighting, dying ; yes, and bearing hunger and thirst—up to a point. It flames up and it can also die down ; it is not an element a leader can induce by the reason, but one that he must closely watch whenever he is called upon to take a decision, whose indications must be divined in the blood. It is very risky to seek to influence this feeling through the reason ; for country, too, is a religion, and only faith works miracles. To appeal to reason in such a matter is to make the first step to demoralization. It is faith only that created all power that ever was. A sound opinion finds many advocates, but no martyrs.

There must be conviction to lay the indispensable corner-stone of victory. Without it no war can be won against an enemy who is to be taken seriously ; it would be against nature and not worth a thought, if that could be. Certainly, a clear line must be preserved by strict discipline, and on the other hand the men must know that everything is done for them that hard times permit. On the top of that it follows that, among real men, what counts is deeds, not words ; and then it comes of itself, when such are the relations between the men and their leaders, that instead of opposition there is harmony between them. The leader is merely the clearer expression of the common will and an example in life and death. And there is no science in all this. It is a practical quality, the simple manly commonsense that is native to a sound and vigorous race.

Where, however, the inborn solidarity that welds the masses in one to fight for their country has been lost, there is no help to be found in artificial measures ;

for the power of advertisement does not extend to moral values. A great empire in which the inner conviction and sense of right that every citizen carries in his heart no longer exist, may perhaps keep the field for a certain time by means of well-paid and adventure-loving mercenaries—but it can never have a national army again.

I feel now, as I said, as if I had been in the trenches for months. The company spends six days in the forward zone, two in the main support line, which is provided with well-built dugouts, and four days more in rest on the embankment at Achiet, where we picked up our guide. We are ending our first spell in the forward zone to-morrow. It is naturally the most fatiguing—for only a few guards are posted in the main support line. With little deviation I spend the day in the following manner :

Schüddekopf wakes me at about five on his return from Puisieux, to whose outskirts the cooker brings coffee, water, ' portions,' and the letters every morning. I jump up and go straight out into the trench. My helmet filled with water, a tumbler, and my washing apparatus are already set out on a ledge. After washing I sit down on the bench and drink my coffee at lesiure. Unfortunately there is little to be said for it. Nor is the ' portion ' very bewitching. Lately we have been given a paste of ground flesh-fibre to eat with our bread. All the same it is a slight improvement on the yellow fat, monkey-fat we used to call it, that we had previously—extracted, as I have heard, from the heads of herrings. One has, in any case, to be very cautious with it ; for the huge glistening flies in their buzzing multitudes are crazy to seize any opportunity to deposit their packets of eggs in it. Even so they have succeeded once or twice already, although I kept it shut up in a glass jar with a screw-top. The only explanation is that they are apparently very enterprising in the use of their ovipositors. It was forced on my notice too on the very first evening that a mouse had been nibbling at my bread. This is one of the incidents that bring a welcome variety to our monotonous existence, and I at once prepared the cunning device that has never failed of success. I laid a bait, and after taking the bullet from a cartridge and shaking most of the powder out I loaded it with a paper bullet and took up a position in the darkest corner of the dugout. The marauder did not keep me waiting long. I took him on the tip of the foresight and laid him out. The news appears to have gone the round among the mice of the neighbourhood, for I have not seen a single one since.

After coffee I light a pipe—from thence on it is seldom out—and look through the letters. That is by far the pleasantest half-hour of the whole day. Letters from home, from the peaceful towns where life goes on in its accustomed round—hard as it is to believe it here ; memories of the last leave—and at once there rises up the blissful vision of a leisurely morning stroll along the cool pavement of a quiet city. The paper comes next. I lose myself in the politics that we here are to develop after the manner of Clausewitz—though by other means. Certainly, when one reads again and again of peace offers and negotiations, one often gets a different impression. Win or lose has got to be the clear issue in a game like this. Besides, we cannot throw ourselves into battle in search of an amicable agreement. When it has got as far as this it means— You or Me.

Usually the shooting begins during the peaceful interval with the post and the paper. Heavy shells pass so high overhead that their flight is heard only as a sharp long-drawn-out sigh ; then the crashes ring out at short intervals in the village and the smoke unfolds between the ruins and climbs high into the air. It is lively too in the wood. Two or three heavy mortar-bombs strike it as though whole mountains were tipped out. Our own artillery hurls an answer back, booming, thunderous reports followed by a shrill and deadly singing that dies away in the distance, perhaps over Fouquevillers or the shattered De la Haie Farm, where enemy batteries are marked on the map. The blunt dull sounds of the hits are borne back on the wind. Between them, the white smoke-puffs of shrapnel, like pinches of cotton wool plucked out and scattered here and there, are followed by the metallic ring of the bursts. The little flashes look perfectly harmless. But any one who has found himself in the spread of their whistling bullets knows that they are dangerous things and admirably adapted for living targets.

Meanwhile brimstone butterflies and chalk-blues flutter above the dugouts and settle on the green ooze of the shell-holes ; and a bevy of larks trill their care-free songs. I, too, sit peacefully on my bench, for I have been so long used to the noise of the front that I notice it as little as the clinking of trams and the hooting of motor cars in a big town. Only now and again, when a particularly violent crash echoes round, I congratulate myself on having got into a safe corner for once. I look back through the long years of the war to the times when we could not make speed enough to get ourselves into the thick of it.

In the meantime Schmidt, the company runner, has been along the trenches and comes back with a rain- and mud-stained book and lays it on the table. This is the report book of the officer on trench duty that is handed over with the Verey-light pistol at each relief. Perhaps, if one or other of those little books came to hand in peace time, it would give a better idea than anything else could what life in the line was really like. Beneath the date and time are laconic notes about the weather, shelling, sounds, activity of the enemy or unusual events in hand—writings that change every two hours. Whoever prizes bare facts, shorn of all literary trimmings—a taste that experience of war very much favours—will here find what he wants. I put together a brief report from these particulars, and the runner takes it as the morning report to battalion headquarters. No surprises come to light as I read, for naturally any event of importance would have been reported to me immediately.

Next I put on my helmet and belt and go into the trenches, where there is any amount to do. Work has to be allotted and inspected, men on guard questioned, and various tours made with the officer and N.C.O. on trench duty. The men are partly engaged in digging, partly sitting in the sun in front of their burrows, mending their things or cleaning their rifles. Of others nothing is to be seen but the nails of their boots ; they

lie in their bunks like bread in the oven and rest after
night guard.

Nearly all of them have young, thin, sunburnt faces,
and clear, keen eyes. Since the introduction of gas-
masks the long beards that many of them wore, apparently in pious memory of their grandfathers of 1871,
have disappeared ; and certainly the clean-shaven
features under the helmet-rim express the strenuous
spirit of the man of to-day a great deal better. I can
scarcely picture a bomber in the critical act of throwing
a bomb wreathed in one of those manes.

This is the time for the General Staff Officers and
specialists to put in an appearance. Gunners bracket,
register, and do their shoots ; a junior medical officer
pays a visit of inspection to the latrines ; the gas-officer
tests the masks, mouth-pieces, and tubing. One has
to have a word with these folk, or if they are superiors,
report to them and escort them as far as the bounds of
the sector. With all this the morning hours fly by.

Often too I visit the platoon and company commanders in the neighbouring sector, with some of
whom I am linked by memories of days gone by. It
is true that owing to the continuous losses new faces
are always appearing, but old ones reappear as they
return from hospital. With these I am always at home
at once—if it is only in a tin Siegfried with thirty centi-
metres of earth over our heads. I have sat with them
in cottage rooms in Lorraine, drunk with them in
Flemish taverns, or spent a wild hour with them in a
Brussels bar ; but I have been able to watch them too
in places where a man's native behaviour cannot be hid,
and where a man is nothing but his naked self. I have

seen them crouching for days together in their shell-holes, or waiting during those moments of strange elation before an attack, when the world gleams in a red and unnatural light. I have seen many of them hit and carried from the field, and I knew that if the wound had been a fatal one they would have died in a fashion that became them. There is no sterner test.

Thus we are linked in experience, in mind, and in blood—what could link us more closely ? There are fine fellows among them, some silent and quiet, others superior and fastidious as though the very mud of the trenches soiled their hands, and others again raw and wild, only fit, one feels, to be among men. But one feeling is in us all. Hence our talk is mostly simple and laconic, as always when feeling binds more closely than reason ; we need few words to make ourselves under-stood. When I think where but for the war I might now be—wedged into a crowded profession, in a peace-time officers' corps, in a club, in cafés, among literary men sharpening each other's bloodless wits, I feel that after half a year of it I should have made hay of the whole business and gone to the Congo or Brazil, or any-where else where nature is still untamed. Here we have the war that includes so much else. It educates one in the comradeship of men, and sets in their right place again values that were half forgotten, because there was no opportunity for their expression. One is conscious again of the blood in one's veins, of fate and future rolled in one.

Meanwhile the sun is straight above the trenches and bakes them to suffocation. I am tired out with going all over the place and long for my dugout. I am a good

distance from it and make my way back through a maze
of intersecting and abandoned trenches.   It is not easy
to find one's way about.   It needs a sense of direction
that is only acquired by degrees.   Arrived at last I
drink the cold coffee left over from the morning and eat
a piece of bread.   Then I lay a blanket down in the big
shell-hole near by, for it is my rule to pass the midday
rest in having a sun bath ; though there is the danger
that I may have to take to my heels in a very informal
garb if a few shells come over unexpectedly.

When it is a little cooler I sit down to my table and
compile a dossier whose textual matter is concerned
with administrative affairs, rations, leave, letters to the
relations of the fallen, and similar matters.   This
dossier is sent up the line from the company orderly-
room with the cooker and goes back in the evening.

Then I write my own memoranda in all comfort,
read, or kill time till evening over various, often child-
ish, occupations, like the mouse-hunt.   Once, for
example, I built all the empty bottles I could find into
a huge pyramid and then bombarded it with heavy
English Mills bombs.   The explosions sounded like
the collapse of a china shop.   Or I take the powder
out of the Verey-light cartridges and make fireworks
with it and some paper.   If the uproar is excessive,
Schüddekopf the Silent sticks his flaxen head mis-
trustfully, like a disturbed mole, out of his bunk, where
he has spent the whole morning asleep.

At sunset, when the back areas begin to be heavily
shelled and a last scout circles among shrapnel puffs over
our front, I make another short tour of the trench where
there is now a stir of life.   The ration-party is getting

ready to move off, and soon the first night guards will turn out. There is a slight nervousness in the air, not because anything out of the ordinary is to be expected, but because from long experience we have a keener alertness in our pulses at this hour. All is in order, so I go back to the dugout to write the evening report.

The times for sending in reports are very convenient here. Often we have to make four in the twenty-four hours and two of them in the middle of the night. This reminds me of a veteran who found this extremely annoying. He has been a prisoner in England for a long time now. One night he sat down and wrote : ' Still nothing fresh to report of the enemy. Only a machine-gun is tapping faintly. A gentle clink of glasses in the company commander's dugout.'

When it is pitch dark and one can scarcely see the sides of the trench, Schüddekopf turns up with the dixies. He often comes through a few shells on the way, but nothing is ever upset ; for it takes a lot to disturb his calm. After my meal I climb out into the open above the dugout, near which there is an alarm post, and take a look over the dark expanses. The Verey lights are in full array. Now and then a machine-gun hammers out, and a string of shots whistle shrill and swift through the grass. On every side are men in ambush, and the night hangs threateningly and hostile over the earth. As usual I look out for the friendly beams of Orion. There he is—I hope we shall see each other again in the winter. Then I get down and turn in and roll myself in the grass on my bunk, pulling the blanket over my head to protect myself from crumbling earth and noxious insects.

I fall into a wild sleep, enlivened and haunted by extravagant dreams such as come of such surroundings. Sometimes I wake with a start and hear the sighing track of shells high up and heavy dull thumps in the darkness. Perhaps, back there, they are stampeding the team of an ammunition column, perhaps there are men flattening themselves in the dust. I light a cigarette and see this sorry hole, this forlorn and abandoned cavity whose sides I can touch by stretching out my arms, lit up by the flicker of the match. But the country outside—it is horrible and menacing ; over it the war harries its wearied multitudes ; and though this tiny refuge lies exposed and defenceless in the open plain, still it gives me a sense of security, because it is the only place where I am at home. And now I regret having shot the mouse the other day. I should be thankful to hear it scratch and rustle. Outside a heavy step comes nearer. That will be Schmidt—come to wake me for my night rounds. I stick my revolver in my belt and go out. The moon has risen. Its white light sucks the colours out of everything and makes every object meaningless and wraps it in a pale and shining web of glass. Each thing is clearly seen, and yet seems to be itself no more. Even Schmidt's face is as white as a death-mask. We set out cautiously. Now and then I speak to one of the men standing silently at their posts. Nothing shows above the shadow of the parapet but the cold reflection on a helmet, or the tip of a bomb, or the loaded rifle. The trench stretches on like a white, ambushed serpent which the least provocation will change into a monster, spitting fire. I go beyond the right flank into the unoccupied length of trench that separates us from the neighbouring unit. That is why I have Schmidt with me ; for he must back me up with bombs if we come on an enemy patrol prowling about on the chance of a scrap. But when I stand still to listen, nothing stirs. I hear only my own breathing and the waving of the grasses, and the distant shots from the Copse. I can go back to sleep again.

But very likely I am no longer sleepy, for in this existence I have long since lost the sense of orderly hours. I lie down when I am tired and do not hesitate to get up at any hour of the night I choose. Then I keep the candle burning and take out one of the books that Schüddekopf put in my haversack. The book, too, at such an hour and in such a spot, is not its ordinary self. Its contents have no importance and no reality for me. It reads like a strange dream which has no meaning for me owing to the grip of a stronger and more adventurous life. And yet I have read a great deal in these years, more perhaps than I should have done otherwise. At the same time I have read more with the blood than with the brain ; and I have had the distinction between words and deeds forced upon me—and this would never have been vouchsafed me otherwise.

THE morning tour of the trench was accompanied by a few stray shells. One gets used to them again by degrees, though one can never get entirely used to them any more than to freezing or having teeth pulled out, or any other unpleasant sensation.

When on leave acquaintances ask the customary question : ' I suppose you take no notice of them now.' One nods assent, so as not to rob them of a pleasant thrill, and also because one knows that they are quite unable to imagine the feelings of a man under heavy fire. But one would hesitate to tell the same yarn to an old soldier, for he knows well enough that even the coolest-blooded are bowled over every time a shell bursts and forced to do Death a reverence, however old an acquaintance he may be.

It is the newcomer who shows a more resolute bearing. I have observed in general that he is at first far less overwhelmed by the bursts than one might expect. It is only when experience has taught him that these things can tear tree trunks to matchwood, fling stone walls into the air, or slice a brain-pan like a cabbage stalk, that he learns caution. Each one of the countless sanguinary experiences of which, in due course, he is a witness, engraves itself in his memory, and the sum of these impressions starts to life each time that he hears the howl of an approaching shell. Danger, and the idea of death connected with it, come to him through the ear, not through the eye, and so take on a vaguer and more threatening aspect.

Time and time again he learns to distinguish among the hubbub the one sound that endangers him, and the first whisper that heralds a shell gives him its whole trajectory. He gets to know the risky times and places, and at last becomes one of those war-tried beings who wind their way unnoticed like snakes through the fissured landscape, always on the alert with ear and eye, like an animal whose caution increases as he leaves his lair further behind him. His nerves get more on edge, but at the same time he is more adaptable and purposeful, and as long as he has the vitality he responds to every demand that the warfare of to-day makes upon its soldiers. This caution that finds out the best way with a kind of night-walking certainty through a maze of uncertainty is the only explanation why such countless numbers of shots are expended for one that ever finds a target.

One hit in ten thousand—this rough calculation is in every soldier's mind every time he stands once more in sight of the shell-shot plain, where brown vortices of earth rise and fall amid drifting swathes of smoke, and whistling and bursting pieces of iron fill the air with their pitiless music. But what good are calculations? Among all the ten thousand possibilities the excited fancy hits on, that one alone will perhaps be fatal. Not till then the man of courage says to himself: ' All the same, now for it. It 'll soon get better.' And it is this hope that spurs him forward.

All these reflections that flash every day through a hundred thousand brains vary naturally according to race and temperament, and they form one of the unseen factors that underlie the casualty list. I consider, for example, the Frenchman better at movements under fire, the German and the Englishman at standing his ground under it. A white race in closer touch with nature, like the Canadians, will bring stronger nerves to the business, but the Canadian has not the uncanny elasticity of spirit that reaches almost the pitch of a disease in the modern city-dweller ; while the nigger is out of the running altogether, for he is an utter stranger to the spirit of all that passes here. Any one who has given more than superficial thought to the circumstances of battle to-day is not surprised to find that it is the man of Central Europe, by whom the best machines are made, that also stands up to them best when they are in operation. The hardiest sons of the war, the men who lead the storm-troop, and manipulate the tank, the aeroplane, and the submarine, are pre-eminent in technical accomplishment ; and it is these picked examples of dare-devil courage that represent the modern state in battle. These men of first-rate qualities with real blood in their veins, courageous, intelligent, accustomed to serve the machine, and yet its superior at the same time, are the men, too, who show up best in the trench and among the shell-holes.

There is one circumstance, certainly, that has a stimulating influence and makes the courage that faces explosives a courage of its own. There are things that cannot be avoided and must be gone through, like an operation, an unpleasant talk, or a fight hand to hand. Under shell-fire, on the other hand, one can rely entirely on one's luck and get through, perhaps, without even a scratch.   You fling yourself into it with the same impulse as when you stake your all on a card— provided you have the temperament.   This brings in the element of sport and gambling, two things that are very closely allied.

In the memoirs of the French general, Marbot, a book that every soldier ought to read, he describes how he stood on a stone platform from which the wounded were being carried every moment during a siege, for no other reason, as he says, but to enjoy the horrible pleasure of letting the cannon-balls rush past him.

There is this disposition in nearly everybody, and I observe it every day in men who, when they come off some duty or fatigue, cannot say enough in describing their last hairbreadth escape.   Only, since most of them have not the daring of a Marbot, they enjoy the excitement after, rather than during the event.   And, to be sure, since his day, death has been given a more frightful aspect than in the days of black powder and round bumbling cannon-balls, when Goethe could acquaint himself very comfortably with the smell of powder at Valmy.   (During my last leave I looked up the passage in question in the *Campaign in France*, and reading it with the eye of experience, I could tell that it, too, was based on a genuine and strong emotion.)

To-day the fever of battle is more like a delirium, and its impressions so violent that there is no room left for observing them.   This is another of the facts that will soon be forgotten if only because the front-line soldier will find few to speak for him ; but they are none the less important.   The generation before the war could not allow any sun to set nor any love to rise unless the brain had more to say to it than the heart. If we are candid, we must admit that the emotions of that time which by good luck we only skirted before plunging, almost as children, into a stronger and wilder one, were nothing but literary sentiments, effusions at second hand, mere reflections of genuine feeling that could not warm the blood, nor make the heart stand still, nor a breath be drawn more quickly. Here one is forced to deeper and undivided emotion, though it be only of a surging, overwhelming terror of which the security of town life gives one no conception.

And the attack, the fighting hand to hand, and the proud and reckless moments when life and death are at stake—all this is bound to transform a generation habituated to them in act. The forces let loose here will change their aims, but the breath of native and primitive life will be there even under the veil of peace. Our life to-morrow will go to another tune. The spirit, like the Phoenix, rushes to annihilation in fire and blood, to rise again in gleaming plumage.

In the evening we were relieved and occupied the main support line, where we are to remain only two short days. As it is only a few hundred metres behind the front line the relief was a small matter. We are in well-built dugouts and need only a few look-out posts.

I am in hopes of finding the cases of influenza diminishing. It is a pleasure to be able to move about more freely. I am thinking of taking a look round Puisieux in the quiet morning hours and escaping awhile from the trenches. Properly speaking we are nearer the danger line here than in the front line, since we are detailed as reserve troops for Copse 125. There has been an infernal and unceasing racket there during the last few days, and if we are called on, our place here will be taken by a company moving up out of the village.

FROM the village of Puisieux a long trench runs in a north-westerly direction. For some distance it follows the road from Puisieux to Hébuterne, which has been ploughed up by countless direct hits ; it then bends off to the right and ends in Copse 125, after intersecting the support line, as well as many other trenches strong and weak. It is called Puisieux Alley, and is so called to show that it is a communication, not a battle trench. That is shown too by the bends and turns of its serpent-like course. Its only purpose is to get one forward, and its windings are no more than are needed to limit the range of a shrapnel burst. But it is without the deep traverses that triple the length of a battle trench and each pair of which encloses a little stronghold. It is without the parapet and fire-step, revetted and hung with weapons, and it is without the massive parados, that casts its shadow like a mountain into the depths of the trench. Hence it does not cast that dark and iron spell that is peculiar to the battle trench.

However, by night it too has a dreary look, for it is one of the great life channels of the front that are shown on the enemy's maps as blue veins or red arteries. Wherever it is laced in a network of other trenches, wherever a conspicuous tree stands up as a landmark, or wherever it reaches the highest point of a small rise of ground, there are simple figures recorded on the map, and these figures, linked in turn to others, hang on the concrete walls of the artillery dugout on the other side. The artillery officer on duty, who gets these figures on the telephone and takes his two angles of fire from them, has no idea where he throws his lumps of metal when he blazes off. But over here, when they pitch and flame up, a heavily laden platoon, that imagined the relief safely over, scatters in all directions ; or a carrying party throws down the rolls of wire and the corrugated iron in a hurry and creeps into the little holes that here and there are broken away in the sides of the trench. Perhaps, too, two men are just passing along who carry a long strange bundle from a pole passed over their shoulders, with two waxen yellow hands protruding from the wrapping. They feel the burden of death that they carry already on their own heels and drop it and run blindly away along a forsaken sap, where they find the shaft of an old mouldering dugout, and there they wait panting, till it is quiet again outside and they can go back to recover him who has done with fear as with life.

Yes, any one may be glad in the night time when he has this alley behind him. He makes such haste that he pushes past the dark figure that he meets without a word, though it would be likely enough for two men meeting in such a spot to exchange a word with one another. It is better in the trenches, for there you know at least what to expect, but here you never know from one moment to the next.

But with the first light of dawn, when the ration-parties set off for the village, the picture changes. They go over the open, for they prefer the straight path trodden in the grass to the winding trench below it, where at every moment the dixies knock against the sides. They are glad enough, too, after a sleepless night, to step out freely in the open ; but if some shells come over they jump down as fast as mice dart for their holes when the buzzard circles above them. They make little of the rifle bullets that pass over at random, for it is still too dark for an enemy outpost to see them. When, however, they pass the same way on their return an hour later a string of machine-gun bullets patters so ominously near them, throwing up little spurts of dust right among them, that there is no question whom they are meant for. Now they have no choice but the trench, for while they talked it has become full daylight. However, they have already cheered the eyes of the machine-gunner over yonder, sitting bored and half asleep behind his gun. He puts a cross on his map and the time beside it, and next morning the ration-party is surprised to find itself shot to blazes. They lose three men and arrive without their dixies.

As soon as the sun is high in the sky the communication trench lies deserted, for man has become a night animal and shows himself by day only in the great moments of battle. Up in the western sky there is an observation balloon—a faint yellow patch just about over Bus-les-Artois—and yet from this height every slightest movement can be seen and armed scouts, too, spy out the communication trench. They see nothing, however, but a runner perhaps, or a single officer or a wounded man limping to the dressing-station. Otherwise all is quiet—only tansy and yarrow nod their clusters over the edge of the trench and the plantain holds its tiny mace erect where the road once ran. The cry of the partridge shrills out on every side from the grass : fat beetles that have fallen into the trench flounder through the loose sand, and the crested lark takes its bath in the shell-holes, where the soil has so soon become friable again, undisturbed by the shrapnel charge scattering over the ground and burying its bullets into the hard-trodden floor of the trench.

I generally make some use of this favourite hour of the day, and this morning took a stroll to Copse 125 ; for it is as well to have a quiet look at the place where at any moment one may be thrown into the battle. Uncertainty of one's ground is a heavy handicap at such moments, and by doing away with it one gains a great advantage over the attack. As it ' was shooting '—this expression is a good example of the impersonal way we accept the enemy almost like the weather—and as, too, I had plenty of time, I sat down half-way on a big tussock that had slipped down into the trench and had breakfast and observed the insects. Then I put up my knife that, like a backwoodsman, I find it convenient to carry in a sheath stitched in my breeches, and continued my pilgrimage to the ill-famed copse of which I have already been told so much.

I must say the sight of it is not very cheerful. Shell upon shell has torn up the chalk, over which in any case there was only a thin layer of black humus, and a white powder has settled over what miserable traces of the undergrowth remain, so that they look as pale and sickly as if they had grown in a cellar. Roots and torn-up beeches and severed branches are thrown together in a coil—often hanging over the battered trenches, so that one has to pass by on all fours. The mighty trunks of the timber-trees, if not levelled with the ground, are docked of their tops, stripped of their bark and sapwood ; only the hard, battered core remains in an army of bare masts, as though devoured by some horrible cancerous disease. I tried to picture the scene to myself as we may so easily experience it— this petrified wood by night lit by Verey lights, whose white shine turns the bleached undergrowth to a garden of ghostly flora, fixed and fabulous; and among the great bare poles, that every moment throw their shadows at a different angle, flash after flash of a fight with bombs and machine-guns, fought with an insensate desperation that only this stark and epic landscape could inspire.

For here some awful spirit has struck out all redundancy and created a background worthy of a tragedy that far exceeds the pitch of any poet. Hence man has no choice but to become a bit of nature, subjected to its inscrutable decrees and used as a thing of blood and sinew, tooth and claw. To-morrow, perhaps, men of two civilized countries will meet in battle on this strip of land ; and the proof that it must happen is that it does. For otherwise we should have stopped it long ago, as we have stopped sacrificing to Wotan, torturing on the rack, burning witches, or grasping red-hot iron to invoke the decision of God. But we have never stopped it and never shall, because war is not the law of one age or civilization, but of eternal nature itself, out of which every civilization proceeds, and into which it must sink again if it is not hard enough to withstand the iron ordeal.

For this reason those who seek to abolish war by

civilized means are just as ridiculous as those ascetics who preach against propagation in order to usher in the millennium. They form the belated rearguard of an enlightenment that sought to dispose by the intellect of matters that draw their life from a depth beyond its reach. But they are the real pests of civilization though they have it always on their lips. Wherever they are left undisturbed at their work, there civilization emits the first scent of decay. May they ever be a laughing-stock to the youth of our land. The blood shall circle in it fresh and earthy as the sap of a wood in spring and beat with as manly a pulse as in the veins of our forefathers who made a saint of the Messiah. Rather than be weak and timorous, let us be hard and merciless on ourselves and on others. Because we think in this way that becomes us best we here have made ourselves its living example, and shall so continue till the end of the war and after. As long as we have a youth that stands for all that is strong and manly our future is assured.

This was the song sung to me in the wood, though it has not a rustling twig left and though not a bird makes its home there. But men make their home there who are inured to the frightful scene and to the endurance of what surpasses imagination. They come from where the gables bear crossed skulls of horses and where the night of the Solstice is still holy. To forget is not easy in their country where the red sea of heather licks the shallow furrow of the plough, and where the barren stretches bear nothing but juniper and blocks of granite, just as it did in the days when, on the Aller, over four thousand Franks were slaughtered who

would hear nothing of new gods.   Liberty is native to
the land of Widukind and Henry the Lion.   No tyrant
lays his hand on the fields of buckwheat where the
crumbling soil is streaked with the silver of the heath
sand.   Hence it is that one can see in these men to-day
that they come of good stock, and I, too, am proud that
my great-grandfather lived as a free peasant among the
heather.   Stark nature with which they have to wrestle
and the lonely gazing over waste land have fashioned
a resolute and serious race, conscious of an inborn
strength.   For the soul is like an animal that takes on
the colouring of the ground it lives upon.   This hard
and pitiless landscape of the war, too, will brand
those who are strong enough not to be crushed
beneath its impress with an imprint that will never be
erased.   Long hence, when young trees are growing
here and the plough has passed over shell-hole and
trench, this landscape will show in the eyes of any that
survive it.

I have seen many a shell-shot wood, Delville, and
St. Pierre Vaast, and the great Houthulst Forest up in
Flanders which, in the course of a few days, was shot
to splinters, but in none was the sight so horrible as
here.   It reminds me most of Trônes Wood, whose
mutilated stumps stuck out of the ground in front of
us during the days at Guillemont.   It may be because
this isolated patch of wood rises sharply from a bare
plain and so draws the fire from all sides.   For this
reason it would be advisable, perhaps, to leave it unoccupied, and upon the threat of an attack to add such
a weight of shell-fire to the enemy's that no living being
could exist in it ; or else after blowing up its defences

to isolate it in a pall of deadly and heavy gas. For such places are man-traps and their continuous occupation is very costly. That has not been done and there are reasons, doubtless. It is entrusted to a company who have a heavy task though a well-defined one. When I had gathered a first impression I made use of the time to make a thorough inspection of the place. I soon came on a N.C.O. on trench duty who warned me of spots that were exposed at close range to the enemy observation, so that it was certain death to cross them. As I was only the other day, when visiting another company, within an ace of destruction in this more than annoying way—for I went up to a block that was not forty metres from an English post—I was very glad of the warning and asked the man to show me round. He was a Fähnrich who had only been out a few weeks, so he undertook the task with an enthusiasm that was of great service to me.

The shape of the wood is roughly a square, with a few small projections. Just about where its diagonals would intersect is a huge dugout excavated in the chalk. From this branch out a number of tracks and trenches that end in the front line. This line follows three sides of the wood which juts out in a sharp angle towards the enemy. The trench—a mere ditch, often filled in and scarcely recognizable—is occupied by day. By night the posts are pushed forward into the shell-hole area in front—a proceeding that calls each night for extreme wariness and has already cost many casualties, since the English too during those hours occupy scattered shell-holes that are not easy to locate. Hence, prisoners have been taken on both sides. Unpleasant, however, as their plight is in being sent into the un-known, they have at least the advantage of escaping the bursts of shell-fire that descend upon the wood every hour during the night. In the morning they have to keep lynx eyes on the sky, for if there is the least glimmer of light they do not get back alive. Never-theless the Fähnrich told me that his company com-mander, Lieutenant B., had not long ago managed to creep in broad daylight, accompanied by one or two others, into the English trench in order to take a prisoner.

I wished to make the acquaintance of this valiant captain of the post who joined the regiment recently while I was away with my last wound ; so we went back to the deep dugout along a small sap—sometimes on hands and knees, sometimes crouching low. It would be impossible without this dugout to think of holding on to the Copse for a day. There are four entrances, each from a different direction and sur-rounded like rabbit burrows with the excavated earth. These passages or shafts descend at a gradient that enabled those who made them, and who no doubt are dead long ago, to dispense with steps. Cross-bars are pegged into the ground so that the occupants can run up without delay and without slipping, for here every second counts.

When the wood is heavily shelled every living being instinctively makes a bee-line for this spot, where alone it is still possible to survive. The strictest orders forbid any man posted in the line to do so : but here there are no regulations and no front line but what a man makes for himself. It is only because the right men are here that the Copse is still in our possession. Otherwise it would have been lost long ago, for in the last resort it is a good heart that decides a battle, not rules and regulations. The great moment of battle comes to each, officer and man, never as a formula that he has already mastered, but as an isolated case that he instinctively seizes or that he succumbs to. Of the most strapping recruit and of the most competent of staff officers it can only be said that he has learned everything except what cannot be taught. A state expresses its will and power in the training given to its army in peace time, but war alone can show whether its will is embodied, and therefore justified, in the courage and readiness for sacrifice and strength of resolution of its citizens.

It was this deep dugout that explained to me how there could be any living thing in the wood, for it often appeared from further back as nothing but a chaos of smoke and earth rising in fountains high above the trees. At these moments the whole garrison crouched and crowded in the narrow galleries of the dugout, which were often enough blocked by direct hits and then had to be opened up again with axes and spades. Only the outposts lie meanwhile in their shell-holes, but everything is drowned in tumult and no one knows whether they are still alive or already dead. It is true that a Verey light shot low either from the wood or back to it means, ' Hallo, we 're still here,' but the signal betrays too much to be used often, and the officer in command of the advanced posts is more concerned with his front and near neighbourhood than with his rear.

Thus attention has to be focussed exclusively for the moment when the fire slackens and moves its iron barrier on over the wood. For then it is known whether the enemy is staking material only, or men as well ; whether he means to annihilate only or to take possession too. Earlier on, this moment was distinguished from those that went before by the stillness that preceded a hurricane. To-day, after many a sanguinary lesson, the enemy tries every means to disguise it. He makes the shell-fire ebb and flow again and again in great waves with the aim of wearing us down and taking us off our guard ; he sends over shrapnel in a curtain that explodes over the heads of the attacking troops but discharges its bullets far in front of them ; he shoots off duds, delay-action shells, and smoke bombs that, without exploding, have a demoralizing effect ; and he hopes in this way to deprive the defence of the least breathing space and to launch the attack as closely on the heels of the bombardment as lightning after thunder.

For it has been proved here that man can bear more than was believed and grows in proportion as his resources increase. His powers of resistance leave him always victor in the race with material. And so it will always be so long as he is the master and not the slave of his creations. But if materialism were to make further progress, pacifism too would enter on golden days, for then the mere menace of the better armed would decide the weaker to climb down. Then in truth reason and material, not feeling and blood, would always be the deciding factors—if only for this reason alone, that they would then be the issues of every question.

But here and now the man is still the deciding factor. Here it is still necessary that, when material resources have done their worst and utmost, the best and bravest hearts shall turn the scales. This little wood, or bit of copse, has no importance, and its name, if it had one, would never be heard of ; the holding or losing it is a mere grain of sand in the balance of the war—but all the same I wish I may have one day the power and opportunity to say what was done at such spots and what the men were who stood their ground there. For no words and no thanks can be enough.

I found Lieutenant B. the sort of man I expected—a type that, thank God, is not infrequent here : few words, a powerful fist, and an open heart. The troop of light-haired, foolhardy, and good-natured soldiers of fortune who invaded Italy under Frundsberger and gave the Swiss a trouncing at Pavia must have looked like this—' armed with long pike and battle-axe in one ' —mad devils and good fellows both. There is a pride in their very bones that forces them to lay about them for what they hold to be the right; and this, after a period of living and letting live, has a really refreshing effect. They hate the French like poison and try to argue themselves into a hatred of the English that does not quite come off. They like best to stay in their own country ; for they have the stamp of their race very clearly marked, and even at home democracy and civilized minds instinctively turn from them. They can but be proud of it.

B. appeared to have had a large parcel sent him and was just at breakfast, and I did not need much persuasion to join him.   He also took a bottle out of a recess hewn in the chalk and a box of cigars ; and so I passed a very pleasant hour with him.   I soon saw he was the man on whom everything hung.   True, he told me that his motto—' Show me your back and I 'll show you my teeth '—had never needed to be put into effect with his men, for they could not be a better lot.   Nevertheless I could see that he was at the back of that too.

I asked him of course about the patrol I had heard of from the Fähnrich.   He told me that a few days ago he crept into the English trench accompanied by Lieutenant K. and his batman.   They chose midday for the job, and that is easily understood when one knows the abundance of shell-holes and the state of mind of the posts at this hour as they lean, wearied with the heat, against the parapet and think of anything but the dead shimmering expanses that lie before them, utterly deserted week after week.   Naturally, then, this hour of general lassitude was the one to choose for stalking. But it is as bold a venture as it is an obvious one, and hence is seldom undertaken.

This time, at any rate, the calculation was borne out. They got into the English trench without being seen and hid in a small overgrown sap.   Very soon after, too, a single man, probably a relief, came by.   However, just as they were about to jump on him, he turned about—put on the alert perhaps by some faint noise or perhaps merely by a sense of uneasiness—saw them, and almost at the same moment threw a bomb. Though B. shot him at once with his revolver there was nothing left for it but to use the initial confusion in order to reach their own trench as fast as possible.

One can imagine the astonishment when three men suddenly stood up as large as life where nothing but death is to be seen. Big game, indeed, and there is only the surprise to thank that they were not stretched out in the space of a few seconds. They were lucky too in getting back before the noise of the rifle-fire brought machine-guns into action. Only Lieutenant K., just as he was jumping from the parapet into the trench that encircles the copse, got a shot that tore his tunic and carried away his left nipple. The oddity of this shot was enlarged upon by the victim of it, as he sat with us at the table, in the same dry tone in which presumably before the war he used to expound Livy to his form; for he was a schoolmaster, and a long thin fellow too.

These little experiences make a good story, and I have often heard them told in most exciting style ; but I find that what it means to be involved in them defies a complete expression. Those are the moments when you come upon men face to face without a shred of cover. A shudder goes through the nerves that cannot even be compared with any other emotion. Even our remotest ancestors who still fought with gigantic beasts must have felt that man himself was a different kind of opponent ; and we, too, inured as we are week after week to horrors of every sort, find that the encounter with men is the sternest test of all. It is here always that the first signs of a decline in the fighting spirit are to be seen. A body of men may be fit to carry on machine war long after they have lost the power to face hand-to-hand fighting. Machinery cannot win a war, though a war is won by means of it —and that is a very different matter.

Thoroughly pleased with my walk, that scarcely a shell had disturbed, I strolled back to the support line. I shall be glad to go to the help of the fellows in front there if the need arises.

I WOULD advise anybody who takes part in a war or any other unusual experience for a long period, to keep a consecutive diary, if it be only a succession of jottings which serve later on to give memory its clues. Such records have a value even for posterity, for it is only thus that the line of fate, still for us the secret of the future, can be recognized; for then the passions of to-day will have no more than a historical importance. In this way a number of written monuments are fashioned which add to family tradition and to the sense of one's country's destiny. This would be of service to people at large; for they have too little history in them, too little feeling for the higher social responsibility that lays less emphasis on the passing individual and his small concerns than on the race in whose history the individual is no more than an organic link binding the future with the past.

Apart from this, memoranda of this kind have an immediate personal value. They force the writer of them to seize upon the essence of his experiences and to get above—if only for a few minutes a day—the familiar surroundings and to put himself in the position of a spectator. The daily experience will appear in a new light, just as a well-known landscape changes as soon as you try to sketch it. And lastly, there is a certain comfort to be derived from even the simplest representation of things, a release through expression;

and in this sense a diary is a confession, a confidence made to oneself.

As things are, nearly every volunteer goes to the front with a notebook, of which a page or two perhaps is written up before it is left behind in some billet after the first battle. I have often seen them. In some of them is to be read in large letters on the front page 'War Diary'; and after that a few notes, addresses, card scores, and a lot else scribbled during the kit-inspections. I hope at least that letters from the front will be kept by the relations who receive them. It takes more energy than one might think to put a few facts together day by day when it is not a matter of life and death. I myself have made time for it, without missing a day scarcely, during the last year or two, though certainly I do not lay claim to extraordinary energy on that account. It is from inclination. Sometimes I am afraid I do too much of it, for nothing is more repulsive to me than the literary man who must immediately display every emotion and every experience to its best advantage and stick it on paper. I hate those fellows and cannot forgive the time when I took their trash for true coin. We have turned the leaves of their botanists' collections of desiccated feelings often enough, and we have no wish to add to these treasures. And if we survive the war, may the temper to which we are accustomed preserve us from writing a line to which we are not driven by an inward compulsion. For us — there will be more important work to do.

In any case the effort to observe goes with the habit of making notes, and when a man is in a situation like this that only these few years can offer and that can never recur in the same form, he ought to keep his eyes open and try to seize its unique features. For this reason I am making use of the second day in the support line for a visit to Puisieux village, though I have to leave some one else in charge and also to upset a great game of Doublehead that was to have taken place in my dugout. I shall be able to play Doublehead often enough later on when I have to take care of the rheumatics that the eternal downpour of the trenches puts into one's bones.

The weather was superb. I took only a gas-mask and a stick and wore a cap instead of a helmet. Once more I was in Puisieux Alley, though I followed it in the opposite direction, and left it half-way as soon as the remains of a hedge gave me the first opportunity to go over the open under cover and to see the lie of the land.

All was quiet. Only two airmen were buzzing off surrounded by shrapnel bursts. Their Lewis-guns tapped away so remotely and their movements looked so smart and elegant that I was envious of the clean and detached kind of war they had of it. They have much to be thankful for compared with us. Above all they can see results with their own eyes. They don't need to shoot away in the vague and lie in ambush months together for an unseen foe. They see their enemy before them not as a force known only by its effects, but as an armed combatant of man and machine. Only in the realm of air is the duel still possible to-day, and with it the chivalry that here below had to die out from the days of great armies, since it is always only the quality of the few. In their case, when one of them has to land owing to a wound or engine trouble, he is received by the enemy as a friend and honoured as a man. He is near to them ; they are bound up with him in a common sympathy that will one day overcome war and make available to man an element hitherto beyond his reach. The masses have to be inflamed with hatred, for it is not within their power to annihilate the foe whom they honour—the highest expression of war, however, is aimed not at men but at the idea behind them.

There is another thing I envy the airman. War is not for him as for us a daily wearisome labour. For him it is a sport that offers a short fierce trial of strength. So I could follow with my mind's eye the two that went over my head and then parted company, and see them landing far behind the front on a green field, leaving their machines to the mechanics and throwing themselves into easy chairs, having breakfast and reading the paper.

I do not grudge it them, for every time they go up they risk their lives. But they have an easier time than we have, as they themselves admit.

I went on along a winding foot-track leading through the double layer of shell-holes that surrounds the village. When we evacuated this area after the Somme battle there was not one miserable blade of grass left. The battlefield extended on all sides as naked as a bit of the Sahara. But though the innumerable shells had scorched and torn up every root, millions of seeds lay concealed in the ground and at once began to cover the unploughed earth once more with thick turf. Then when the spring offensive of 1918 came to a stop at this same spot, the guns began upon.it afresh. The shells fell here and there at first, but soon the green carpet was branded more and more thickly and the brown soil turned up. The number of shell-shot waggons was another indication that the offensive had been held up here. They were strewn about in fragments and the carcases of teams were already beginning to crumble into lime. It is no wonder, either, that this devastated, trackless stretch of country, traversed by trenches and wire entanglements, afforded a mighty bulwark to the defence. It was a bold thought to renew the attack over this desert.

The scene was the same in the village too. Overturned limbers on the edge of the village street, the iron all mangled and warped ; great heaps of empty ammunition baskets, shot-riddled helmets, broken rifles, tattered packs—all the debris and scrap of a great offensive, which an iron fist had brought to a standstill at this spot, joined with the ruins of the houses in blocking the narrow roads. Among it all, and looking perfectly meaningless, lay the various apparatus of peaceful life—a plough, a broken soup-ladle and a Nativity of wood, with its gilt washed off by the rain. Direct hits had torn up the red-brick paving of the paths, and others had burnt-black and sulphur-yellow marks on bits of wall left standing.

It was a depressing experience to stand alone among these slag-heaps. I climbed over the ruins of what was once a farm to reach the garden and went carefully forward, for I know the danger of the deep wells hereabouts when their tops have been torn away and the opening grown over. Many a one has felt the ground give beneath him in these villages, and either been drowned or fallen a prey with broken limbs to the rats that always haunt such places.

The solitude of the gardens, that lay as though enchanted in the glare of the sun, made a friendlier impression. When human dwellings are laid waste horror is soon at home there. A cold exhalation rises from them as from open graves. The destruction of a happiness that can never return touches the feelings of all who pass by. Nature, on the other hand, teaches one that the essence of life is in continual change, not in what is unique and irreplaceable. Nature, that scatters ten thousand seeds that one perhaps may germinate, cares nothing for this man or that. His destruction is a paltry matter. Near me I see a pear-tree whose trunk has been broken off by a shell, but from the stump there is a sheaf of young shoots. Its withered crown is garlanded with convolvulus and adorned with a diadem of white cups. In the middle of the vegetable garden a deep shell-hole is half-filled with water and coloured by a green and living slime and a host of larvae. And there, where the garden soil lies firm and even, weeds have sprung up and carry on a relentless struggle for light and air. The thistle whose leaves seem cut out of metal, the rank dandelion and the ox-eye daisy are all in the pride of their strength and have almost crowded out the less hardy cultivated plants. Here and there a cabbage still survives, and true to form shoots up its great flowered stem. A rose-tree struggles aloft above the thicket of weeds, but the effort costs it so much that its blooms are sparse and poor.   Its life is menaced of a sudden on the very spot where it stood well tended and without care.   It is well that it has not forgotten its primeval force and the art of bringing forth its double flowers.   It will often be able to bloom again, but once it is crushed to earth in a time like this, all is over for ever.

Thus all around I saw the plants taking possession of the ground.   They hung down over the old shell-holes.   Camomile, currant, wallflower had taken refuge in the ruins.   Nettles had stormed the heaps of debris, and the paving of the garden paths was sunk in gold-brown cushions of moss.   And I thought to myself that if our ears could hear this wild struggle for life and increase, a tumult would rise up in this peaceful garden that would drown the fiercest battle of men.

Next I crept through a hole bored through a wall by a shell and found myself suddenly in another world. It was a graveyard upon which desolation had descended like the Last Judgment.   In the Dresden gallery there is a celebrated Ruysdael, ' The Jewish Cemetery '—a picture that I have often stood and looked at.   It always seemed to me that the master was conscious in this picture of a great rift between the meaning of death and the importance that men give it.   Nature is repre-sented in sullen wrath over the stone monuments with which man would like to perpetuate his personality. A like thought came to me here too, where every broken cross seemed to cry out : ' There is no eternal rest.   There is only eternal movement, that presses every smallest particle into its service.'

Only a moment ago this thought had been clothed in

a garment of foliage, and been instinct with a wild elation. Here it presented itself as oppressively and horribly as that myth of the Wandering Jew who can never find peace and travels this wretched world century after century under the curse of perpetual unrest. There are two phases of being. The one says Yes and the other No.

The grave-stones were cracked, the iron crosses broken, the copperplates on which names and pious texts were engraved were riddled with shrapnel bullets and rolled up like leaves. Heavy stone slabs with armorial bearings and inscriptions had been torn from their places by the force of explosions and broken in half ; in the vaults they had covered, the fragments of metal coffins and wreaths of black glass beads were strewn about. In the middle of the cemetery, near a fallen angel, rose the dark cone of a cypress that had by an odd chance come off unscathed. The ranks of children's graves were turned up as though by beasts of prey and the porcelain plaques that had stood at their heads were flung in all directions. Rats had burrowed everywhere and dragged mouldering remnants into the light. Upon an overturned block of granite there was chiselled the announcement : ' Concession à perpétuité '—a painful gibe at man and his place in Time.

I was glad to leave this caricature of a cemetery behind me, and turned next to the highest point of the village to see the church as well. There was nothing of it left but the materials of which it had been built. A heavy round pillar that lay half buried in this slag-heap of masonry suggested that it had been in the

Romanesque style. That is very possible, as the villages of this district are very old.

The spot where I stood commanded a wide view. Behind the white ground-plan of the village which lay in the hollow like an excavated settlement I saw on the opposite slope the brownish-green expanse of shell-holes over which I had come. Communication trenches led out fanwise towards the wide network of the front which disappeared to right and left in the glare of the midday heat. Although the view excluded extended far behind the enemy's lines, the whole country was utterly deserted as far as the eye could see. Isolated clouds of smoke that rose up here and there as though propelled by some hidden force of nature increased the sense of desolation.

Suddenly black smoke ascended as though from a crater field in an extinct planet, and after a while the sound of a heavy crash was carried across and then followed, by a strange inversion, the howl of the heavy shell before it struck. If any one had been standing there he would have had not a second to take cover, for the shell had travelled faster than the noise of its passage through the air. When the broad smoke-cloud dispersed it revealed a group of bare poles and showed me that it was Copse 125 that was under fire. Next, salvoes of shrapnel flashed out in quick succession over the tops of the naked trunks, tiny whirling points of flame that sent out white balls of smoke with a sound as gentle as the report of a pop-gun.

What went on over there, far away from where I stood, at one point in the whole length of the long front, looked harmless and trifling enough ; and it seemed odd to me that this patch of wood had made so strong an impression on me the day before. And I suppose that if there were a mighty being who could take in at one glance all that went on from the Alps to the sea, it would appear like a battlefield of ants, or like a gold-beater's hammer beating out one single minute piece of work. We, however, who are aware of only one part at a time, are overwhelmed by our own particular destinies and see death in awful shape. We can scarcely imagine that what happens here is linked up with a vast scheme—that the threads at which we tug, in apparently senseless contradiction of each other, are somewhere connected together in one single plan.

FOR two days we have been in rest at Achiet embankment. At least it is always called the embankment, though really it is a deep cutting that traverses the bare and undulating country. In its sides, overgrown with thick bushes, are roomy dugouts extending along the face of the slope. I have chosen a little blockhouse situated on the level ground, although I was warned against it because a few days ago a sergeant-major was hit there by a shell splinter. But in the first place I have a desire for fresh air and light after the time spent in dugouts, and I am ready to risk a good deal for this indulgence ; and also I have a superstition that places which have once been unlucky are safer than others. I am very pleased with my dwelling-place. It is hidden away among the bushes, dry, weather-tight, and built of snug, well-seasoned timber. Close by are some semicircular iron huts dating from the days when the English were here.

There is little to be said of the surroundings. There are the same low and treeless hills and hollows as usual. Close to us is the anchorage-place of a large captive balloon. Yesterday we saw its occupant jump out at the approach of an English airman. There was a strong wind and the parachute dragged him some distance along the ground. Nevertheless he landed safely. There are a number of tanks to be seen round about with their engines put out of action. Achiet village is quite close. It is in ruins, but not much shelled, and so its walls are thickly overgrown and the flat white discs of the elder adorn them in thousands. We are not much shelled here, but, to make up, what we do get are from a big naval gun, that shoots on a flat trajectory with quite incredible fury. Probably we owe this torment to a long-range gun that is brought up every night on the railway lines. Sometimes too we have bombs, dropped wide of the mark as a rule ; but the other day one landed disastrously in the middle of the crowd round a regimental band.

Our days pass here very pleasantly. Our duties are wisely limited to the minimum. It is not as it was in the early days, when the amount of training put in during the days of rest almost passes belief. Training ought to be like a prayer : short and earnest. Nothing in this respect is more mischievous than exaggeration. The men know how to use their arms. They use them every day in the line. The important thing is that short and strenuous reverence be paid to the spirit of discipline. Three things keep a body of troops in fighting form : fighting spirit, strength, and discipline. Fighting spirit—as I have said before—is the least easy to influence. It is the great prerequisite and justification of war—the spirit of the race and of the blood pledged to the last drop. There lie the roots of the strength whose full development is dependent on outward conditions, fresh air, nourishment, clothing, and a lot else. When this soil fails fighting spirit is like a seedling planted in arenaceous quartz—it goes on growing for a while of its own resources and then gives out. It is a tragic destiny when a great enterprise comes to grief from this cause. Finally, the purpose of discipline is to economize and direct the other two elements so that they are brought to bear on one aim with overwhelming force. It is a means, not an end ; it is in seeing it in its true proportion that the real fighter is distinguished from the soldier. It is one of the danger-points of the Prussian system that it easily loses sight of the spirit in the letter and of real strength in the empty show of it. One of the most terrible apparitions is the sheer drill-master—a machine that goes by clockwork. It is bound to break down for the mere reason that in war there is no rule but the exception. The people showed their sound sense before the war when they rebelled against this mechanical spirit of the drill-yard and held it up to ridicule on more than one painful occasion.

To-day, however, as I said, only the bare necessities are required of us, and rightly, for when you have to do with the men it is soon seen that their fatigue is alarming. Many are still in their growing years, and, as the scanty rations cannot be improved, the only thing is to give them plenty of rest so as to husband their strength for the actual tasks of war. Nearly all of them, besides, have influenza still in their bones, and naturally they have less power to resist it than they would have under better conditions. This is the explanation of quite young fellows dying off in the hospitals, going out like candles because they have no physical reserves. This is the omen under which the war as a whole now stands—we are living on our reserves. And the general desire is that the issue, whether of victory or defeat, may shoot up in one flame rather than drag on in this way.

'There are trifling indications that make one think. I had arranged a game of football for this afternoon. Till lately the men were always eager to play. This time they were slack. The ball went languidly to and fro. The forwards would not follow it up and several times the game was only resumed at my order. The men were not fit for it. In this way the hour was got through somehow, for to break off the game would have meant condoning a weakness that must certainly be borne in mind for the future but not on any account openly given way to. It shall not happen again. It will be better to have the drill only, for nothing is worse than compulsory play or compulsory singing. The men become conscious of the incongruity, and a mood is simulated that is not really there. They can sleep in the afternoons or go for walks, or even play cards, for all I care, if they want to. After the drill they can lie in the grass or be given instruction, or we will go into the country to look at the tanks. This is a state of affairs of which much could be said.

And so long as there is beer in the canteen, and possibly Schnaps enough too, a great carousal is held in the huts. Then they can tell each other tales till the ears of the divisional chaplain back in Quéant tingle, and make such an uproar that the English at Hébuterne think an offensive is being launched. Then they will sing of their own accord till the earth rocks—not the patriotic songs that are to be found in school song-books, but that fine song of the Merry Tinker, of the crocodile that wagged its tail, of the son called Waldemar because he was in the wood, the sorrowful ballad of the girl of Hamburg, of the hundred thousand men that went to the manœuvres, and the fine verses about 'Jan Hinnerk ut de Lammer-Lammer-straat, kann maken wat hei will!' Then the temperance league will get busy, Schüddekopf will furbish up his old story again of how at St. Christ one day a direct hit got the latrine, and Sergeant Meier, who as a rule never speaks three words in a day, will come out with his one joke that we all know long ago by heart. And lastly, I myself must be got back to my hut with the greatest care and undressed, so that they can say next day: ' Did you see the Lieutenant ? He was in good form as usual.'

Yes, yes, much that is irregular will take place there and, if it gets known, I shall have to swallow a sharp reprimand concerning proper behaviour with lower ranks. For it is true—at least up to a quarter of a year ago—that scarcely a day went by when I was not reminded that I had still a great deal to learn. That is true enough. I know it myself and try to improve too ; and it may be the way of the army to let me know it in so cut-and-dried a manner. All the same it does not raise my morale, and I can after all lay claim to morale, if it is conceded to the man in the ranks. I will readily yield my place and give precedence to better men, but there does not seem at the moment to be great eagerness to step to the front. It is only among the staff that I have felt suddenly that I was too young and ought to make way for an older man. But imagine a man who was good enough to fight and yet could not feel himself worthy of any rank whatever ! Over and over again from safe quarters behind the line one hears it arrogantly stated that things go badly because the company officer is too young, and exactly the opposite is the case. The canker with us is that no room is made for ability. The organization is certainly magnificent, but it is so much organization that the force of personality has no sphere of action. Quite apart from the paltry matter of my own case—can a man with us (unless he is one of the famous one-year volunteers), a workman, if you like—to speak plainly—become an officer ? Old warrant-officers under some circumstances are made lieutenants in the Landwehr, and that is the one miserable concession.

The officer must be a gentleman according to the often-quoted saying of Washington. But is the one-year volunteer a gentleman ? Such was never the interpretation Washington intended. A gentleman is one whose activities are directed to ideal, not material aims, and such men are found in all ranks. One only needs to hear of all that nowadays passes as education for the word to leave a bad taste in the mouth for ever after. And it is exactly the profession of an officer that in contrast to every other encourages a consideration for moral qualities rather than the rational sciences. It calls for a real education that is not limited to the brain merely, and in this way a people can make for itself a nursery of representative and unprejudiced manhood ; and if the selection is made from the strength of all the nation one cannot imagine an element better calculated to bind the whole. All honour too to a good upbringing and good manners—but in these days it does not really matter whether a man eats with his knife or not. We live in a time when even more important considerations and · scruples have to be disregarded.

When equal sacrifices are required, equal rights must be given likewise. This has been such a commonplace of thought for a hundred and twenty years that one is ashamed to find it still in need of emphasis. In any case, if this principle is applied in an army, and the great saying about the Marshal's baton that every recruit carries in his knapsack is not a mere empty phrase, everybody feels that he is in his place, whether he is born to command or to obey. If I give any offence by this, I may add that this would be an army composed entirely of Fahnenjunker.

Democratic sentiments ? I hate democracy as I do the plague—besides, the democratic ideal of an army would be one consisting entirely, not of Fahnenjunker, but of officers with lax discipline and great personal liberty. For my taste, on the contrary, and for that of young Germans in general to-day, an army could not be too iron, too dictatorial, and too absolute—but if it is to be so, then there must be a system of promotion that is not sheltered behind any sort of privilege, but opened up to the keenest competition.

If we are to come to grief in this war it can only be from moral causes ; for materially, whatever any one may say, we are strong enough. And the decisive factor will be the defects of leadership ; or to express it more accurately, the relation in which officers and men stand to each other. It would not be for the first time in our experience, and it would be another proof that peoples too (for it is on the shoulders of the whole people, not of the ruling class) always repeat the same mistakes just as individuals do. The battle of Jena is an instance. This defeat should not be regarded as a great disaster, but as a just and well-deserved warning of fate to cut loose from an impossible state of affairs ; for in that battle a new principle of leadership encountered and overthrew an antiquated one. Every war that is lost is lost deservedly. One must always bear that in mind if one wishes to be the winner.

I spend my times off duty in the most varied ways. The first morning, of course, I rode over to the baths of Sapignies with clean clothes in my saddle-bag. Quite close lies Cagnicourt, where the great offensive began on 21st March of this year—an incident that new experiences have already buried far in the past. I took a strange and melancholy pleasure in following on horseback the course over which, on that first day of the attack, I was driven by a wild enthusiasm. First I found a large grave and over twenty crosses inscribed with names I knew well. It marked the place where that ill-fated shell went up—one that none of us who by a miracle survived it will ever forget. Finally I came to that murderous spot where I got my wound on the 22nd and did not know in the fury of fighting at close quarters till half an hour later that I had been hit. A distance of five kilometres was covered in thirty-six hours—but what those hours cost in will and emotion can never be repaid. They flew by like an opium dream in which landscapes open and things happen that defy all description.

I cannot ride every day, for the horses have to be spared and they too are on short rations. I often go for a walk with Dohmeyer, Sprenger or others whom I have known a long while. We look for partridge eggs or old fuses to shoot at—a sport at which the other day a man was severely wounded. Near the embankment, in the direction of Ablainzeville, there is a large camp of huts abandoned by the English. It is surrounded by large rubbish heaps. Stacks of shells and cartridges were left behind. We go there every afternoon for a great rat-hunt. We shake the powder from the cartridges into their holes and light it. Rats as large and fat as guinea-pigs pour out and are either shot with revolvers or killed with sticks. There is nothing much, then, of interest to record.

Every evening we play cards in my hut. Money has no meaning here but to be won and lost at cards. Meanwhile we wage war on influenza, that is to say we swallow large quantities of a spirit with the strange name of Ober-Ost and an even stranger taste. Some affirm that it is a wood spirit because after a few glasses it acts as a complete narcotic. Here Dohmeyer is in his element. His enthusiasm takes dangerous forms. Last night he riddled warrant-officer K.'s long boots (they share a dugout) with revolver shots, in the belief apparently that he was rat-hunting.

I MUST mention the airmen once more, for a school friend whose existence I had half forgotten and who now belongs to a celebrated scout squadron, heard I was in his neighbourhood and invited me to a little festival yesterday evening.

I was taken by car from Achiet and driven to a château where the aerodrome is. The dinner was given by the squadron commander to celebrate his twentieth victorious combat. I was given a very cordial reception in spite of the characteristic rivalry that has developed between the infantry and the Air Force, owing to the claim each makes to having the more dangerous job. We got on remarkably well. I was only once pulled up when I spoke of ' going to Paris,' for these fellows do not ' go.' They know nothing but ' flying '—a vaunt that I find very proper. For the rest I was surprised to find there was an *esprit de corps* and a spontaneous comradeship amongst them such as one would expect only from an old tradition. The spirit that animates them must be a very strong one to have achieved so marked an expression in so short a time. A spirit like that has its own future within it, and I feel sure this type of man, once called into activity by the war, is capable of playing a leading part in the Europe of to-morrow whether in peace or war. Something new is going forward here that is easier to imagine than describe ; or rather something new and predestined finds here a starting-point from which it will proceed and develop.   And I would even say that it will achieve a development that will make the political, social, and moral ideas of the latter half of last century appear strange and perhaps barbarous.

I am not speaking of these men themselves, of whom scarcely one will survive the war, but of a new manifestation of mankind which I, in the grip perhaps of a fixed idea, believe that I have encountered more and more frequently precisely in the last year or two.   Just because I know that a man does not as a rule survive his enrolment with it for more than half a year, and so has only a brief acquaintance with his kindred spirits, I was all the more surprised by its homogeneous form and the strength of the spirit that must be its shaping force.

Who, then, are these men ?   It is clear that they are less conscious than any one of their own significance.   Otherwise their protagonists would not write the stuff they do, in stock phrases only fit to be cooked up again by war correspondents.   That is just the best of them.   They cannot write and do not need to.   Enough will soon be written of them.   Their life is blood not ink, deeds not reflections.   Their part is to make history, not literature.   And later, perhaps, when after the war the current of life flows in other channels, the saying of Nietzsche will be borne out by one or other of them :   ' Write with blood and you will find that blood is spirit.'

They are like flame kindled from the mighty army that lies before them under continual fire.   They are a band picked out by the impulse towards ever bolder and more exciting forms of war.   There are cavalrymen among them, hard-riding fellows whose blasé features stare in goggles.   They got tired of waiting in villages and country houses behind the line for the advance to begin again.   One can see in them that they belong to a race that has had mounted warfare in its blood for centuries, and that they look down upon all this business of motor transport and automatic guns as something not in their line.   But there are others, too, who have been reared in the centres of modern industry and are true representatives of the new century.   Young fellows of twenty whose faces have the imprint of hard fact.   The ardour of speed, the tempo of the manufactory, the poetry of steel and reinforced concrete have been the natural surroundings of their childhood. Wealthy, proud young fellows brought up to work by their fathers and sent in the holidays to Bavaria to shoot, or to Kiel to yacht.   Technical science is a joke to them.   They have their aeroplanes under control as a bushman his boomerang.   They are thoroughly accustomed to the enhancement of life by the machine.

Yet all are bound together by the high tension of action, by that fighting spirit which has perhaps its strongest expression in those little communities.   The game of life and death is a sport to them and the players are esteemed according to their coolness.   Battle is not only their duty, but the keystone of a particular kind of life which they strive to embody in its extremest form and for which they have been prepared by an upbringing in feudal, national and military circles. The inevitable climax is a decadence, or, rather, a dandyishness that is in strange contrast with the frightful strength it masks.   When they sit together in light open coats and the white collars and bow-ties that they habitually wear, in spite of the annoyance they cause in the army, they discuss the prospect of life and death with the same frivolity as the chevaliers of the *ancien régime* discussed love. This recklessness, so often indulged in words that only the simplest expressions of it escape being ridiculous, is sharpened into paradox and pointed by cynicism just as happens in the case of every great and long-enjoyed passion.

Yes, battle is their great passion, the joy of challenging fate and of being fate themselves. They feel this when, after taking off, they cast themselves into the unknown as a whirring flight of eagles. When they soar to a height from which the front appears as a thin network beneath them, and they themselves are visible in the trenches only as a succession of dots, they are filled with the sense of hitherto unimagined daring and of invading entirely new territories of feeling. It is their fortune to try their strength against the picked manhood of the whole world in a new dimension, in unbounded space and amid the ever-shifting scenery of the clouds. They know that only one of two possibilities awaits them ; and hence every encounter is inspired by the fury of desperate animals. And yet there is more than a blind pugnacity in these circlings, these sprays and jets of tracer bullets, in these banks, in the pursuits prolonged almost to the very earth, these steep dives, loops, and spins. The crisis of the battle cannot find its vent in the muscular system. It has to be transmitted to a delicate machinery in cool blood. This calls for a race with brains of steel above hearts of fire. To this is due the triumph with which they soar above the enemy machine when, in flames and dismembered by the rush of air, it falls headlong to the earth—a feeling of incomparable intensity. This sense of power is what urges all who know it to go up again into the clouds.

Another thing that makes the contrast more emphatic is the attractive shape in which death appears to them. They have no week-long marches, no grubbing about in mud and putrefaction and blood. They know nothing of battle by night and in mist, and of limbs shot away. They throw away their cigarettes, climb into the cockpit with clean uniform and snow-white linen and carefully tended hands, and in one hour they are back again.

It is a matter of good form when talking after a flight to stick to the purely technical details of the adventure without embarking upon feelings like a servant girl who has seen a ghost. When some one says that he lost control at two thousand feet and only flattened out just above the ground, every one knows what that means. It is always pleasant to live among people with whom there is no need to explain one's feelings.

It often happens that one of them does not get back. That is arranged for after the fashion of soldiers. It is a custom to leave a sum as a deposit for one's own obsequies. This was the way of our ancestors. A good carousal is the best celebration of the dead. What matter if the fallen man is not in the circle where change alone is invariable ?

We to-day are not such materialists to make anxious talk of it. We leave that to those who tremble for their lives, because they feel in themselves nothing but mortality. Yet, every time that a flying-man falls as a burning brand to earth, a nobler issue is answered than that of being or not being.

SINCE last night I have been in the line again, in my doorless summer dwelling. Old K., now in command of the 2nd company, with whom only fourteen days ago I passed some happy hours in Hanover, was my predecessor. After I had taken over, we sat an hour together on the bench in the pitch-dark hole and rejoiced ourselves with the little jokes that seem particularly brilliant in such surroundings. It often occurs to us that only a journey in a D train, half a day in a restaurant-car, separates us from the large, well-lit towns. And so from that we come to the conclusion that death seems least terrible against a background of happiness, and that we would rather die in spring when life is decked out gaily than in winter. We men of to-day are keyed up to a high pitch. The same energy that refracts our life in the roaring towns into a thousand colours makes our battles terrible. It is just when life is menaced by death that its earthly light shows up most brilliantly, as in Boccaccio's pictures of it outside the gates of plague-stricken Florence, as in the love of consumptives, or as a Bacchanal on a sinking ship.

I am always glad when a relief is carried out without casualties. Nearly every time it takes its toll, and the annoying part is that not a blow is struck in return. Many a military treatise might be written on the problem of movement behind the line. This time we were lucky, though I passed an unpleasant moment a few steps from Puisieux.

One of the pleasantest privileges of command of which I avail myself as far as possible is that of going by oneself during these movements of troops. I always set off a little later so as to find the relief completed when I reach the front line.

Just in front of the embankment I came on a very comic scene, though in truth it was no laughing matter. An artillery detachment was making use of the moonlit night to mow the grass in a hollow. The men at work with their horses and waggons showed against the sky like a group cut out in paper with scissors. Just as I got past them in the valley without misadventure, a volley of light shells fell among them, and in a moment men and horses vanished like wraiths. Only the outline of an overturned waggon showed against the horizon.

Next, when I had reached the main road to Puisieux, I saw that heavy shells were falling at fairly short intervals just outside it. The reverberations rolled for long through the valley. I felt uneasy in the desolate scene and hastened to get past this nasty spot, which I could not avoid without getting among the overgrown gardens with their hidden wells, barbed-wire fences, and open cellars. I had naturally taken note of the interval between the shells, and I decided to get as near as I could to the danger point and there await the next one before making a dash for the dressing-station dugout at the edge of the village. There I would look out for the next volley before running through the village into the cover of Puisieux Alley. It would all have gone right, but that in my first dash I lost my map-case ; and I was very unwilling to abandon it, particularly as I had taken it from an English artillery officer's dugout in the great offensive. I had just recovered it when the roar of the approaching shells sounded high over the village, and I had only time to crouch behind the stump of a wayside tree that was splintered like a huge shaving brush. Three of them landed with a crashing explosion in the valley, already filled with smoke, and the fourth pitched in the road and went up in a blaze, hurling road-metal and splinters on all sides. Though, of course, it was too late I tried to leap to the far side of the stump, and losing my balance fell into the ditch among the dried branches of the tree. When I reached the dugout, which was only a few steps away, I came on the body of a man in the middle of the road lying with outstretched arms. It was the Verey-light post, who had perhaps been hit some while before, and who appeared to have rolled down on to the road from the place where he had been stationed in front of the dugout. I jumped down the steps and found the medical officer of another regiment who was on duty there. As soon as I told him he had the man brought down.

' Nothing to be done,' he said at the first glance, and one did not need to be a doctor to see that. A large splinter had caught him in the back of the head through the helmet, and the peaceful expression on his face showed that death had been instantaneous. I did not stay long in this carbolized subterranean atmosphere—only long enough to wait for the next lot to come over. Then I got through the village and was thankful when I could run like a mole into the Puisieux trenches. And I was just as thankful too that I had not to follow them as far as Copse 125, which looked like a blazing cauldron, but could turn off to the right for sector A, where calm prevailed.

IT must be recorded that to-day August Schüddekopf whistled. I heard him while, still in ill-
humour and fatigue from the night before, I sat on
the outdoor bench and wondered whether to be pleased
or vexed by the first rays of the sun. And he whistled
that pretty song of the girl who got up early to pick
blackberries. The ration-party brought news first
thing that leave was open again. Schüddekopf is next
on the list, and what that means can scarcely be said.
In any case when a man from Lüneburger Heath begins
to whistle it is as significant as when a Neapolitan
leaves off. It means that he is in a condition of quite
uncommon happiness. If I had a little farm between
Ulzen and Celle and was newly married, like August
Schüddekopf, and could get my pack ready to-night
and go there, I should scarcely know, either, how to
express my feelings. I am heartily glad for his sake,
for since my trusty Winke was wounded in the great
offensive and his successor, the waiter, failed to return
with the ration-party, we two have made a perfect
combination. I talk little and he far less, and so we
get on excellently together. Above all, I know that I
can rely on him. That is worth a lot, for he carries my
rifle and has to be always at my side. His predecessor,
as I more than once had occasion to notice, had an
uncanny faculty of vanishing as nimbly as a monkey
in moments of danger, and when he reappeared again
he was so full of the heroic deeds and adventures that

had come his way in the meanwhile that I felt a wretch beside him. But with August Schüddekopf there is no need to look round. I can always be sure he is close behind me with the same impassive expression on his face. Hence he had my best wishes when, loaded with his pack, he took leave of me at noon to-day.

Fusilier H., who takes his place as my batman while he is away, is quite another sort of fellow. By his bearing I should say he was an intelligent artisan and also a great individualist—a type, therefore, not encouraged with the Prussians. It is well known that with them no one is encouraged very much, and so I can fancy that in peace time he would be seldom out of the guard-room. And even here he may think himself lucky to have come to me, for I can always find something to say for such fellows. There are many of his sort to be found among those who volunteered for the war and who, all the same, have little taste for the daily routine of the army. Hence they are a thorn in the flesh to company sergeant-majors. The officer, to whom fighting is, or ought to be, the essential thing, knows better how to get on with them.

I first got to know H. a year ago when we were in Lorraine. We had been made up to strength by a batch of recruits after the first battle in Flanders. I pride myself in recognizing a man of courage at the first glance, and as soon as I saw H. I had the feeling that he was a man to watch. I had not long to wait for confirmation, though certainly of an unexpected kind. The sergeant-major, who had H.'s conduct sheet in his hand, whispered over my shoulder : ' Not a great catch

this one. One punishment after another. He's been
under arrest as well.'

I was glad, then, when a short while after he reported
as volunteer for a raid that was to penetrate deep into
the French lines. I took him, though I had plenty to
choose from, and many nearly wept when they were
left out. As it turned out, I did right. The show went
as badly as it well could. We did not take a single
prisoner and left nearly all our men either dead or
wounded in the hands of the enemy. H. too was
counted missing, but half an hour later he suddenly
turned up, lugging a machine-gun which he had
captured on his own. I had a lot of unpleasantness
to bear and the affair was duly noticed in the French
Army Report. This machine-gun was the only con-
solation in the whole sorry affair. From that day on
our friendship began—though not a word was said of
it ; and, indeed, it had for me more than one dark side.

I will pass over the little but almost daily difficulties
that one pig-headed fellow can get one into when he
gets across all his superiors in turn. I should long ago
have attempted to get rid of him, and the frequent
transfers gave opportunities ; but some fighting or
other always cropped up meanwhile, and at once he
showed up at his best. I thought, too, of putting him
under confinement a few times ; but in the long run
there is no use in beating a man down. Any one can
do that. The point is to make use of his qualities.

Once when we were in rest before the great offensive
I said one day during training that a time was coming
when we should have to fight all day long in open order,
and made the comparison of a great battue when one

breakfasted on the move and allowed nothing whatever to upset one's composure. When, after this, I gave the order to march, the Commanding Officer rode up to me and asked : ' One moment. Is it your practice to allow your men to smoke pipes on duty ? '

It was H. of course. He had his rifle slung, his hands in his pockets, his pipe in his mouth—just as if he was out shooting. Now when one considers the stress laid particularly by the officer in higher command upon infusing into army drill a dash of fighting spirit, and that he is always telling the soldier to use his imagination and adapt himself to the situation, H. had really had a stroke of genius. That this was his own opinion I could see from the injured face he made when I told him off in a fury. He had really only wanted to show me that he alone thoroughly understood me, and that he and I knew how things would go. For to smoke on duty requires the same independence of mind as one must bring to bear upon any deliberate infraction of the established order.

He had done me a bad turn, but given me something to think about too. A day or two later I sent the company out on a wide front in sections, with express permission to smoke and talk, and the one stipulation, that while making for a distant objective they should make the fullest use of every advantage the country offered them. As I rode here and there from one section to another I found that, though they certainly talked, they nearly all went like a troop of Indians on the warpath, adapting their course to the lie of the land.

I do not mean to say that the ideal of the bushranger should be pursued in all cases, but it helps as everything else does that comes more from love than compulsion.   We have to employ other means to-day than in the days of Frederick the Great when the officer, with the whole battle on his own shoulders, took in his serried ranks at one glance.   A leader of troops to-day sees very little of his men in the sea of smoke, and cannot compel them to be heroes if they prefer to live for ever in another sense.   He must be able to rely on them ; and he can only do so if he has trained them to take the initiative rather than to act as puppets who carry out movements at the word of command.   They must certainly be schooled in an iron school if they are to be real men, but they must be taught to face death with a higher sense of their own responsibility than in former days.

We have to free ourselves more and more from drill in massed movements ; for since the development of mechanical weapons the functions of massed troops devolve more and more upon individuals.   The most essential task to-day is to educate the soldier so that he can stand on his own with a machine-gun without losing sight of the engagement as a whole.   We shall be able to replace platoons by machine-guns, companies by tanks, cavalry regiments by air-squadrons, and to rely, indeed, entirely on the machine—but only if we can count upon a high grade of specialist.   For as Xenophon said when he encouraged his infantry to withstand cavalry, ' all that occurs in battle is done by men.'   It is men who win battles, and only the picked men who know how to wield the best weapons.   The materialists—and the supporters of soul-deadening drill are among the worst and the most abandoned of them—must never be allowed to forget it. As soon as ever we can put into battle large bodies of men of the same type as the flying men whom I visited the day before yesterday, resolute, intelligent, bold, and capable of enthusiasm—as I confidently expect from the further development of our people—we shall no longer need what we understand to-day by drill. There will be so much of interest to learn that no time will be left for it. Obedience will, of course, still be the first duty of a soldier, but I must be greatly mistaken if such men are not most disposed of all to be obedient, seeing that they have the best of all foundations of it in their own convictions. A man who feels that an extreme responsibility rests upon him will always strive to do his best.

To return to H., who does very little to honour such an ideal of the future. However, it is just of the young artisan that much can be expected. He is not, it is true, bound up with the country like the peasant by tradition and by the very soil, but, on the other hand, as a child of the industrial cities, he is adaptable and easily inspired with enthusiasm if he is taken the right way. There are mighty energies to be aroused in him, and a state that does not know how to mobilize them and harness them to its aims of aggrandizement will never dispose of the impetus required by the terrible exertions of modern war. It may be admitted that fine talk will not go far with him. The artisan must confront such an enterprise as a free agent, and not as a coolie who lets himself be shot at any moment without any inward conviction. If we lose this war every single individual will have to set his teeth ; hence it is only fair,

if we win it, that every single individual shall profit. Men
go to war, after all, for some object in which, whether
it is of a spiritual or material kind, they have some share.

One morning before the great offensive opened,
shortly after the affair of the pipe, the sergeant-major
appeared as usual to make his report. He had another
disappointment for me over H.

' I have also to report that Fusilier H. disappeared
yesterday evening, leaving his pack behind, and was
still absent this morning from parade.'

This was said very solemnly as though it was the
final conclusion of a long-standing difference of opinion ;
nor could I help feeling myself that this news was a
painful defeat. There is a delightful but quite forgotten novel called *Spitzbart*, by Schummel, in which
a rector of that name was undone as soon as he was
compelled to put into practice his highly theoretic
system of education. I felt as ridiculous myself that
morning and wished nothing better than that H. had
disappeared for good.

He was, however, brought back after a few days—
from Tourcoing, a town near Lille, where we had been
while on rest a few months before. The company was
engaged on training when he made his appearance, and
even before I saw him I felt the eyes of all upon me
with exulting curiosity. I gave the order to carry on
and went to the rear with the deserter. Although, if
merely for my own interest, I tried every means to
penetrate his reserve, there was nothing more to be
had out of him than that he had got to know a girl
while we were there and found it absolutely necessary
to see her again.

' The devil you did—but have you at least seen for yourself that it must not happen again ? '

' Yes.'

' Then I will tell you something. I had recommended you for the Iron Cross of the first class before I had to send in the report that you were missing. I need not say how damaging that is for both of us. You are guilty of a serious offence and will have to go before the Commanding Officer. I shall not put in a single word on your behalf, but I will tell you a saying that you had best take careful note of : " With loss of honour much is lost. But if you win glory folk will tell another story." '

With this I left him ; but all the same I went at midday to the Commanding Officer, Captain von B., who unhappily was killed a few days after—a man of a true soldier's heart. Thus the matter passed off with a few days' arrest. It would take too long to tell how H. conducted himself in the great battle. His conduct, in any case, bore out the little saying I had told him. And this, after all, is better than if he had passed the time in the cell of a garrison. He was sent back wounded to Germany, and then one day the sergeant-major reported with a wry face : ' H. is here again.' Immediately after, H. himself appeared at my hut as good-hearted and unmilitary as ever. ' I wanted to be with you again.'

He is, as I said, an individualist, and hence for him the person counts for more than the thing. This is the case oftener than one thinks, and therefore, where a system spreads its fixed network too far, it is for the personality of the leader to rescue what might else be lost.   For a system is nothing in itself.   It is only good in so far as it is a form in which personality is developed.

My batman and I have, therefore, already had a varied experience in common.   I even know that he speaks up for me.   When I go along the trench at night I often overhear the talk of the men coming up from their burrows at my feet, and I confess that I am glad enough to eavesdrop a little, for there is much to be learned that otherwise I should never know.   When it is his voice I hear on such occasions, I discover that we two are fabulous beings and the true epitome of the whole company, and that if we were once left to it we should swallow the enemy's trenches a mile at a time.

On the other hand, I sadly suspect that my things will be in very poor order for the next few days, for I have taken him on principally to give him a soft job, since he still suffers from his wound.   Besides that, I need him for a little affair that is to take place the day after to-morrow.

YESTERDAY evening I had a visit from the officer in command of the company on our right. He belongs to another regiment and is called Lieutenant D. He shares with me the defence of the unoccupied length of trench that separates our two sectors. H. had to show what he could do, and brewed a mess-tin of grog over a cooker of solidified spirit. We sat ourselves on the bench out of doors and drank and smoked, and as the heat of the day lingered in the trench we were soon overcome by that pleasant annihilation that the Russian calls the ' third sweat.' The crickets chirped, D. took off his tunic, laid his revolver on the table and remarked that I lived so comfortably, he might be sitting in front of some forester's lodge.

He told me that he had joined the army as a pioneer and then had transferred into the infantry.

At the beginning of the war the pioneers had an important part to play, for their peace training was in any case very largely technical. So they were the first who had to do with hand-bombs and mines, and from their small storm-detachments sent in front of the waves of attacking troops the storm-troop was evolved, that handful of resolute men who fight like a machine, each performing his own task, with the object of making a breach for the troops behind. Later, this part of their activities passed from the pioneers to the infantry, whose two radical functions of fire and movement were therefore developed to a degree that no one could have foreseen. This is another indication of the widening-out of responsibility.

With the beginning of trench warfare, too, the time had come for a real fighting man to find his proper place in the infantry rather than with the pioneers, who were employed more and more on work of construction. Hence I could well understand my guest when he told me of his transfer. He preferred to hear the bullets whistle than to have charge of a pioneers' park behind the line.

There is a saying common among those who wish to lament the bitter fate that forces them to carry on with a safe job far behind the line. It is a very old army saying and has a good ring that has kept many a one in countenance. It is : ' Orders must be carried out.' But to-day it has to run : ' More than is ordered ought to be carried out.' Every one with a job at the base ought to report again and again for service in the line—if he is indispensable he will soon find it out.

Unfortunately, I suspect that these sheep in wolves' clothing who give their poltroonery so heroic a mask will talk big again once the last shot is fired—for they know how to talk. But I will not give my fury rein, though it is no less here than usual. We shall recognize them at the first glance, for the front is a great freemasonry whose members are cemented together with blood more closely than any other bond could cement them. The spirit that is set only on endurance will wilt and fail, but the spirit in which a hundred thousand volunteers fell in front of Ypres will stand because it was bent on doing, not on living. Systems may perish, the empire change, but what was planted here will bear fruit.   The survivors must take on the heritage of the dead.   They must always be hard and never weak. They must have nothing but contempt for him who cannot stake his life for future greatness.   Let us hope they will turn their backs also on those who go hawking their fiercest brand of Prussianism—so long at least as it turns on the flesh and blood of others than themselves. This war tears off all masks and proves once again that the Fatherland owes most to its less distinguished sons.   This must not be too soon forgotten again.

Once more I found in this pioneer the new type that I have mentioned more than once already.   As I said, what is new in it is more easily felt than described. The soldier of to-day differs from the soldier of '70-71, just as we differ from our grandfathers, little as those at home may like to think it.

To say that, is to say all.   A new ardour, a new energy inspires life, and the men who to-day are behind the machine-guns will to-morrow be in industry, carrying their tempo into the markets and the large towns, creating the political situation and giving the world a new face.   It is to be hoped that in peace, too, they will come to the front, for that will be the best for the country.

We passed a happy evening.   I was delighted with my unexpected visitor.   As his tongue loosened he told me of his experiences in that impassive tone that adds a particular force to terrible events.   He knew the front from Alps to sea, and we discovered that we had been at many of the most famous and most fiercely contested points at the same time.   I was particularly fascinated by his account of the times he had passed as pioneer, for he was able to enlighten me about a great deal I was ignorant of till then. I will try to give a specimen in his own words:

'It was at Lens that I first made acquaintance with mines. We were literally day and night on a volcano. There was a close network of coal mines spreading for miles beneath the ground occupied by both sides and connecting them with each other by subterranean galleries. This was very unpleasant for us, for the French had the plans of all the mines in their possession, and so we had to be always on the look-out for patrols who might emerge in our rear from exits of which we knew nothing. From the shaft both sides systematically drove mining galleries beneath the trenches. Almost every day a bit of trench went up in the air, and then there was nothing for it but for both sides to storm the still warm crater while timber and debris descended from the sky. Those who got there first won the day. Meanwhile one had always to have a cigar alight, for at that time we had no bombs with pull-out fuses. There was merely a bit of fuse sticking out, and one held the cigar to it before throwing. You knew them, no doubt. They were tin boxes with a handle, filled with explosive, old nails, and scrap iron. They were heavy and unwieldy, but effective.

'Below we were on day- and night-shift with the mine charge always ready. Sometimes there was a pause for listening. Then we could hear on every side a faint hammering, digging, and picking that got on the nerves more than the howl of shells coming over above ground. Often the sounds were quite close and distinct.   Then we knew that an invisible enemy, stripped to the waist, was working for life and death close beside us.   It was a matter of minutes whether we should scotch him or he us.   Many a time I have crouched with the microphone at my ear waiting for the moment when they got to work on the other side before putting in the dynamite.   As time went on they got more and more cunning.   They had men at work till the last second so as to drown the grinding noise of the heavy charge being pulled along and put in position.   It was like a smoking powder barrel.   You had to be there to realize it.   Once we had only just time to light the fuse and run for it.   The explosion was so powerful that two men at work three hundred metres away in a crossing gallery were killed by the rush of air.

' The day after we had a hectic experience, when we were at work at another point.   Suddenly the soil gave before the pickaxes.   The carbide lamps were buried and a great cavity opened in front of us.   Before we realized what had happened we heard excited voices— we had collided with a French mining party.   We threw ourselves flat on the ground.   There were three of us, myself, then a Fähnrich, and two pioneers stripped to the waist and entirely unarmed.   It was not by any means pleasant.   We could smell cigarette smoke, and there was the unbearable suspense of knowing that there were men ambushed within a few yards of us.   You know those moments before coming face to face with the enemy when you have to gasp and yet don't want even to breathe.   Added to that, it was pitch dark.   I had the feeling—with the massive earth on every side—of lying already in the grave.

' We crouched like that for an hour at least without moving a limb. At last they were fools enough to shoot ; and once I knew where they were I emptied the magazine of my revolver. At that one of the pioneers, a Westphalian miner, sprang forward and laid about with his pickaxe. Next I turned on my pocket torch and we had a look. There had only been two of them and I had hit them both. I could hardly have missed in the narrow tunnel. They were both dead. The pick had finished off one of them.

' This happy ending gave us courage, and feeling curious we decided to explore the passage that had suddenly opened in front of us as in a tale from the Arabian Nights. This moment you will know well enough, too, when one sweats with fear and secretly forswears all deeds of valour for evermore. But once well out of it, courage revives, and later on one makes all possible fun of it. If a man had not this power of forgetfulness, his first battle would assuredly be his last. We crept forward, then, very cautiously, and soon felt a draught of air and heard a peculiar whirring sound in the distance.

' It was clear to me at once that we had made an important discovery. For some time we had suspected the existence of a large subterranean power-station, run by the coal that was close at hand, which supplied light to the French positions and drove the mine-trucks. What we heard must have been the noise of this power-station. The current of air was caused probably by the ventilation shaft that drew the exhausted air from these subterranean and bomb-proof dwellings and works.

' By the light of my torch I made a sketch-map and

then we went back. We dragged the two bodies to our side and then covered them with earth, so that it looked as if the roof of their tunnel had fallen in. The company commander had a good notion when I reported the incident. He got a number of steel-containers full of compressed gas from the army pioneer depôt and the same night they were carried to the spot where we had our encounter. The next morning we went there with a listening apparatus. We had arranged by telephone with the artillery to keep the exits of the shaft under fire at a certain hour. We then partly opened up the hole again and poked the gas-containers through one after another and released the gas. There was no danger for us as the gas was carried forward at once by the ventilator. We could hear its whirring quite distinctly with our listening apparatus. It was not long before what we expected occurred. The sound ceased for a moment and then began afresh. The French, after their first surprise, had reversed the ventilator and tried to drive the gas back about our ears. So we carefully blocked up the hole and breakfasted at our leisure with the ear-phones on our heads. We heard the humming of the engine for about a quarter of an hour longer. Then it died down and all was still. Later we heard from prisoners that we had smoked out the occupants like rats and poisoned the whole shaft for months. Besides this the artillery had inflicted severe losses as the occupants streamed out.'

Thus one thing led to another, till it grew late. I took D. back to his sector as part of my night patrol of the trenches. When I got back they were still sultry

with the heat.   For some reason I felt wrought up.   I
blamed the powerful grog, or the pioneers' tales which
brought to my mind that men sought each other out
not only on the ground, and on and under the sea, and
in the air, but in the very bowels of the earth as well.
But are we not in any case of the breed of Pluto that,
shut off from every joy of existence, hammer away in a
subterranean smithy of the future ?   What we fashion
and whereto we are fashioned ourselves will not be
made clear till far later than we can now imagine.

Perhaps we ourselves will be more astonished than
any when we know.

THIS morning, when I had made the one step that takes me out of my dwelling-place into the midst of nature, I scanned the weather as carefully as a hunter who is going out after buck. After four years on active service one gets the weather into one's very blood. To-day, however, even a city dweller would have seen from the sun, as it came above the horizon as smooth and clear as the blade of a knife, that there was to be another hot and cloudless day. This put me in good humour, for I had something on hand that required perfect visibility and heat enough to induce a drowsy state of mind. To keep myself fresh I did not go as usual along the trench after my wash, but retired again to the dugout where the moist walls of earth kept the air as cool as in a cellar.

There I carefully studied a little map that a section leader had made of a part of our front. It showed a length of trench on our right wing, bordering on the unoccupied sector. The pioneer and I discussed it the night before last. On this flank the trench bellies out in a huge crater. Its sides have been faced up and small tin Siegfrieds driven into them all round. This spot is occupied by the right-wing section of the company. Guard is kept day and night, and every hour a patrol is sent out along the unoccupied bit of trench. Till a few days ago they lived in peace, disturbed by nothing more than an occasional shrapnel shell. One morning, however, the man on guard heard an unusual slow whistling noise and immediately after, before he had time to get clear, down came a black ball as big as a pound weight that fell behind him and at once exploded.

This phenomenon was repeated. Some days only once or twice ; on others one of these balls came over every hour. The annoyance was small but continuous. On one occasion the dixies that had just been put down on the top of the trench were hit and the soup ran out as though out of a watering-can. Another time the section leader's coat, hung out to dry, was burnt and torn ; and finally, one of the patrol that the company to our right sent out every hour to keep touch with us was so severely wounded by a splinter that he had to be carried back to the dressing-station.

The whistling gave sufficient warning, as the descent of the projectile was not very rapid ; but the men had all the same to be always on the alert so as to take cover at the right moment. Their nerves were on edge. They caught themselves together if a bird flew over the trench or a distant shot was fired anywhere along the front. One misty morning they went on the search over the top and succeeded in digging up one or two duds out of the ground.

They were cast-iron cylinders through the centre of which was bored a rifled hole. We have them too. They are grenades fixed on the rifle-muzzle and projected by the force of the rifle-shot. They were introduced when it was found in the course of trench warfare that the infantry had no weapon with which to deal with an enemy at a short distance from their own trench. Before the war a distance of eight hundred

metres was reckoned for, and at this distance, before
the attack with cold steel, rifle-fire ought to be annihilating. But when the opposing forces dug themselves in it was found that the distance between them
might be as little as thirty metres. However furious
the rifle-fire, it swept on harmlessly over the trenches
and spent itself on the ground behind. Hence the
infantry were provided with bombs for the shortest
range, and the rifle-grenade which can be shot up in the
air to drop like a stone behind the enemy's cover, for
longer ones. In this way the use of explosive became
general throughout the army, and fighting at close
quarters more murderous and savage than it had ever
been. Such methods, though not very sporting, are
effective. They mop up the space between two
traverses in the space of a second, and give to a single
man a power that is as far beyond the thrust of a
bayonet or a revolver-shot as the machine-gun is
beyond the muzzle-loader.

I found it hard at first to reconcile myself to these
methods, because I had joined up with quite another
picture of battle in my head ; but I have acquired the
horrid taste for the concentrated force that they put at
one's disposal. This taste of which I am not ashamed
must infect others too, for I have often seen the look
in the eyes of those who broke into the enemy's trenches
with thunder and lightning in their grasp. There is
poetry there too. But it requires nerve.

This continual bombardment from rifle-grenades
was all the more unpleasant because the point from
which it came was concealed by a low rise, and therefore it was impossible to return like with like. Accounts

then would naturally have been squared, as always when one need not merely put up with an annoyance, but can retaliate as well.

I examined the air-photographs with a magnifying glass, but they were so closely pock-marked with shell-holes that nothing could be made out.

It was impossible either to see over the rising ground from any other part of the trench or from the adjoining sector. By standing upright on the top of the trench one would have had a view of the ground beyond the rise and perhaps been able to observe something—but certainly not have lived to tell the tale.

Hence the idea naturally presented itself of creeping up to the post by night to cook their broth for them, or else to approach it very cautiously by daylight and try to snipe one of them. I think I have mentioned already that we are in the midst of the Somme battle-field, and hence our position is linked with the enemy's by a number of fallen-in trenches. One such com-munication trench runs like a hair-parting over the brow of the low hilltop. It is so weathered and crumbled and overgrown that no more is left of it than a flat brown furrow over which the herbage of No-man's-land begins to close in from either side. This furrow seemed to me to be designed for stalking along, and I was so taken with the idea that I decided to put it in action to-day at noon—noon because the posts are then at their drowsiest and no superior officers are likely to come along, for a few nights ago an officer who went out on a raid was not seen again, and for the time there is little eagerness for officers' patrols.

As I said, the weather could not be better, and so at

twelve o'clock I went along to the right wing where I was to leave the trench.   H. came with me to carry my rifle, a short carbine with a telescopic sight attached.

' This is something like,' he said, and I replied : ' More in your line than cleaning puttees,' and I pointed to mine which were coated with mud.   I got him to press the hooks of my sword-belt together so that they should not catch on anything and then un-buckled it, after attaching my revolver to a long knitted woollen cord and putting it in the right-hand pocket of my tunic.   We took off our helmets, for, in spite of the grey surface coating, our manufacturers appear to find no means of preventing them reflecting the sun. Such a discovery would be worth a lot more in my opinion than the discovery, for example, of the reason why we had to invade Belgium.   We did not worry about colouring our faces, for the sun has done that so thoroughly that even at a short distance they melt in with the colour of the ground.

As I had carefully arranged everything with H., we were able to climb out over the parapet as soon as we arrived there.   It all depended upon wriggling like snakes more with our ribs than with our limbs.   At first the trench was a little deeper, but to make up, we had to crawl through the coils of a concertina, that is to say, spirals of barbed wire.   They are easily carried in a bundle and then extended on the spot where they are required.   After that, however, the edges of the trench were no higher than our shoulders, and the flowering grasses were the only cover left us.

It is difficult to describe this feeling of being without cover.   In modern war it is always uncomfortable to feel oneself bereft of armoured-plate or earthwork. Every spot of one's body becomes painfully sensitive from the consciousness that one may be hit anywhere at any moment. This pain is of course imaginary, but not any the less unpleasant on that account. It is the instinct of self-preservation trying to threaten or warn or break down one's courage and fighting spirit. Courage has its answer to give. A continual whisper is audible. ' Get on with it ! You can't be seen. Forward ! Don't be a coward ! '

Thus, even in the fighting man as he creeps forward, a continual fight is raging between two forces—a murmur of warning and inspiriting voices. It depends on the blood whether yes or no gets the uppermost of this excited tumult in the ears.

Gradually our nerves get the better of the situation— one in which we were no mere novices. I made long pauses and then crept forward again, always careful not to move even a stalk of grass from its place. The muddy ground was cracked, and so hot that it almost burned our hands. The acrid scent of the earth was mingled with the aromatic essences of a thousand flowers. It is a smell one notices only when, on hot days like these, one lies like an animal with one's nose to the ground. H. conducted himself very well. I did not hear him make a sound and only felt him when his head pressed against the sole of my boot. In this manner we got along by degrees and at last reached the crest of the rising ground. There we found a recent shell-hole that must have been the result of a shell with a quick-action fuse, for it was as flat as a stork's nest and the grass all round it was burnt black and close like a dirty blanket.   Just in front of it grew a group of thistles covered with purple blooms of a size that I have seen nowhere but here, where the ground has neither been ploughed nor mown for years.

I slowly propelled myself into this shell-hole and brought my eyes on a level with its rim.   I could see nothing at first, and had to get out my knife and cut a thistle stem to make a window.   I had to do it with caution and noiselessly, for the enemy might just as well be two or two hundred metres away.   For the same reason the plant, after the stem had been severed, had to vanish slowly inch by inch.

This done, I had a view.   I saw little, but all I wanted.   Beyond, on the level ground, the enemy trenches stretched without sign of life, their outlines dancing in the heat that flickered over the surface of the ground.   At right angles to the trench that extended to the horizon on either hand, a trench came straight forward and ascended the further slope of the rising ground, ending about thirty metres from us in a block protected by hedgehogs and knife-rests of barbed wire in a tangle, through which the grass had grown tall and rank in a brown and yellow screen.   This spot was no doubt the hostile post.   I had already made up my mind it was the same trench that had provided us with cover for our stalk, only on that side as far as to the post it had been kept in condition instead of being abandoned and almost filled in.   From various spots in the trench we had often pointed rifles in the direction from which the grenades appeared to come over the hill and plotted the intersection of the lines of aim. Hence this supposition had already appeared to be a

probable one.   Now, too, I saw that a night raid would
have had little chance of success, for the trench was so
thickly wired all the way along that without artillery
preparation it was practically unassailable.

All was now clear to me.   Only nothing was to be
seen of the post.   I had reckoned that, feeling utterly
secure, he would have shown his head at least over the
top, but the tangle of wire interwoven with grass concealed the dead end of the trench, where he was probably standing, as impenetrably as a wall.   There was
only one little gap, perhaps two metres wide, a short
way further back, that gave a glimpse into the trench.
Looking from above, the eye fell on one tiny patch of
the hard-trodden mud of the bottom of the trench
before it disappeared behind a bend.   This was all I
could observe ; it did not seem to promise much, and
it might be all there would be till night fell.   But when
one lies in wait for the most dangerous being in the
world, one must spare neither time nor pains.   So I
decided to wait and not to move my eyes once from that
spot.

I got myself settled and drew up one leg a short way
—a signal that H. understood at once, for I felt the
barrel of the carbine being slid along over my ankle.   I
drew it to me, released the safety-catch and adjusted
the back sight ; then lay over on my left side.   The
carbine is a short rifle and its barrel is almost entirely
cased in wood, so there is very little of it to reflect the
sun.   Hence I took the risk of advancing the barrel
with the utmost caution till the muzzle projected beyond
the thistle stems.   All that was left to do was to take
the open spot of the trench floor in the V of the back

sight. Then all was ready. I looked at my wrist-watch and took the time.

If there were really a man on the look-out behind the brown-yellow screen he was certainly as cunning and cautious as a beast of the wild. There was not a clearing of the throat, not a cough, not one of the murmured words or bits of song with which posts are accustomed to while away the tedious hours. There was not even the sound made when a man leaning on the fire-step shifts from one foot to the other. I should have heard it in the noonday stillness and at this short distance for a certainty, and it would have got me like an electric shock. But there was not a movement. Once a grasshopper began to chirp and then, as though alarmed by the noise he made, was still again. Then a swarm of small sky-blue butterflies appeared and played about the thistle heads. I almost believed I could hear the beat of their wings. I heard the ticking of my watch and the sound of the heat as it broke away a crumb of earth from the edge of the shell-hole. There was a dead calm, and yet often a light wave passed over the variegated surface of the ground. It was the heat passing over the earth.

It beat on the skull and made the lock and butt-plate of the rifle burning hot, and glowed on the shell-hole till it was like the hot-plate of a stove. All power of thought began to melt away like wax. But though one's thoughts wandered as they do on the edge of sleep and lost themselves in strange by-paths, yet the will was alert like a wild beast in a landscape over which the clouds are drifting and flocks of birds. If two grass-stalks rubbed against each other or the ear played one false with an imagined sound, up it sprang—the will, and with it fear.

Are we then still aquainted with the soul of the hunter now that no beast is dangerous enough to hold his own ? Hunting has become a sport, a recreation, and a mere reflection of the daring exploit that once it was. Perhaps something of its spirit has passed elsewhere. Something of its hazard and reward are found where high stakes are played for on the tables with money as the counters. For to the genuine gambler the winnings are not the essential thing, but the staking of all on the throw, when loss or gain are knit in one sensation. He engrosses the triumph of the victor and the anguish of the vanquished. Well for him who is not dependent on the gaming-table with its shallow reflections of life and destiny for the experience of such feelings ! In all great passions, whenever love or battle stir the blood, one is conscious not only of oneself but of the other too. One enters upon a higher order of being in these moments of intoxication. The reason is replaced by the blood, and one envisages the person who confronts one, whether it be friend or foe, as another self.

Hence it is that any one who fires at men feels apprehension, however safely ambushed he may be. It is impossible for him to keep calm. He is in a fever of mingled savagery and suspense. This fact admits of many a philosophic and moral formula. For the soldier it is quite simply a repression that must be overcome, and quickly, before a veil falls over the eyes, or the heart bounds, or the finger trembles as it grips the trigger.

In war, instinct and intuition play a great part ; if only because it is a matter of the blood and not of the reason. On this occasion, too, it was more an intuition than a conviction that told me : Behind that grass thicket, motionless as it is in the surrounding desert, there is, all the same, a man in hiding. And though two hours went by, this feeling never left me a second's peace. I was not deceived.

Suddenly a sound rang out—a sound foreign to this noontide scene, an ominous clinking as of a helmet or a bayonet striking against the side of a trench. At the same moment I felt a hand grip my leg and heard a low-breathed whistle behind me. It was H., for he had passed those hours in the same alert tension as I.

I pushed back with my foot to warn him, and at the same moment a greenish-yellow shadow flitted across the exposed spot of trench. It went by like a streak, yet I saw it clearly. It was a tall figure in clay-coloured uniform, with a flat helmet set well down over his fore-head and both hands grasping his rifle, which was slung from his neck by a strap. It must have been the relief as he came from the rear ; and now it could only be a matter of seconds till the man he relieved passed across the same spot. Once more I sighted my rifle on it sharply.

Now at last the time seemed endless. A murmuring of voices arose from behind the screen of grass, broken now and again by suppressed laughter or a soft clanking. Then a tiny puff of smoke ascended—the moment had come when the returning post lit a pipe or cigarette for the way back. And in fact he appeared a moment later, first his helmet only, next his whole figure. He was not so tall as the other—an Irishman, perhaps, or a Londoner. His luck was against him, for just as he came in the line of aim, he turned round and took his cigarette from his mouth—probably to add a word that occurred to him during the few steps he had come. It was his last, for at that moment the iron chain between shoulder, hand, and butt was drawn tight and the patch-pocket on the left side of his tunic was taken as clearly on the fore sight as though it were on the very muzzle of the rifle. Thus the shot took the words from his mouth. I saw him fall, and having seen many fall before this, I knew that he would never get up again. He fell first against the side of the trench and then collapsed into a heap that obeyed the force of life no longer but only the force of gravity.

At the same moment I ducked my head below the rim of the shell-hole and drew back the carbine. It was pulled out of my hand at once. For now it might be our turn if the survivor over there was an old hand at the game. Hence, we tried without turning round to shuffle backwards by the way we had come. Meanwhile a whistle was blown repeatedly as a signal. Then there was a peculiar metallic noise followed by an explosion. There was a puff of smoke above our heads and the dust flew up all round us. It was a rifle-grenade shot so perpendicularly into the air that it had exploded before reaching the ground. Next the bullets of a machine-gun further to the rear began to whip the tall grass, but we had already got over the hill and in a few seconds were in safety in the trench.

I went straight to my dugout without pausing to look round me and threw myself on my bench. There I lay till evening like a man who has a job behind him that has taxed his utmost strength. I smoked one cigarette after another and stared at the smoke that rose to the roof in the dim light and chased the long-legged spiders into their corners. I was glad that I had not relied in vain on my weapon. I have more than once had a misfire or a jam when fighting at close quarters, and the feelings I have experienced have pursued me like examination-fever even into my dreams. It is always the same dream. I see a man coming nearer and nearer, and try as I may to shoot at him, my will has no power over my weapon.

And this time I had not, either, missed my shot, and that for me was not so much a matter of course as the short distance might suggest. For I am sorry to say I do not shoot as a soldier properly ought to, one shot like another, but like an avowed victim of temperament. Sometimes when we are out in rest I fill my pockets with ammunition and am delighted to find that I can hit the smallest mark ; then on range practice with the men I will nearly miss the target altogether.

To-day, however, I knew for certain as soon as I took aim that I should hit.

DURING the night we heard heavy shelling over the wood. The fire was concentrated in short bursts and increased thereby to an elemental fury. Towards morning a thunderstorm, for which heavy masses of cloud had been banking up during the evening, broke over us ; and now we lay in a huge cauldron, over which earth and sky were hammering at once. It reminded me of that memorable day in the battle of the Somme when the Guards stormed Maurepas during a thunderstorm and we among the ruins of Combles thought the world would crack.

I lay half asleep on my bed and hence the uproar made a dreamlike and mysterious impression. A battery started up far away to the left and its hits were all round the dugout. They made the damp ground tremble and the fine dust trickle down the walls. I was so tired that I could only tear myself from sleep for a moment at a time, and when I did it seemed to me that out there in the storm a monstrous beast went to and fro seeking for my retreat in order to tear it to bits like a defenceless bird's-nest. I closed my eyes again ; but the feeling extended to my dreams and my ear heard all that went on. Once the post, who was drenched to the skin, burst in to report that a red Verey light had gone up, and still I lay where I was, glad that I was not the commander of the reserve company and up against it in such weather. Just after, I heard our own artillery break out in a storm of fire that soon ceased again—very likely it was nothing out of the ordinary !

With morning, the scene was grey and cheerless. The storm had noticeably cooled the air. Heavy driven rain was still falling and hung a curtain before the eyes. When H. brought the coffee I heard him wading through pools ankle-deep, and the hanging foliage that sheltered the entrance of the dugout ran in streams. Where the sides of the trench met the grey sky there was nothing to be seen but mist and spurting rain-drops ; the monotonous gurgling was broken only by the splash of clods washed down by the rain, and the migration of half-drowned insects into my shelter was in full swing. As I could feel all my old wounds shooting I was not eager to go out into the wet. I pulled the blanket over me again when I had written out the morning's report. I based it principally upon my own imagination, for the report of the officer on trench duty appeared to have had several duckings and its contents were indecipherable.

Then I poured away the coffee as it tasted of mud and made myself a cup of tea, provided from a canister I had made plunder of during the great offensive—a store which I husbanded carefully. It was the very morning for reading through the ' Sponge '—those lengthy documents mostly of tactical significance, at the head of which is written ' Utmost Despatch.' They are shoved into some corner of the dugout where it is their habit to accumulate in vast heaps. Finally one signs at the foot of them and sends them on to the next company sector, where the same fate awaits them. This is the Paper War. In the course of trench warfare it has assumed immense proportions without greatly endearing itself to the man in the front line.

This time as usual I shook my head as I sat in my hovel, whose roof of earth began already to glisten with drops of water, and applied myself to this literature. It contained little that was new. We have been the children of trench war too long not to know already to what a vast bulk it has grown in the course of years, and when one reads all these minute instructions, extending from the designs of latrines and the collecting of cartridge-cases and corks of bottles to the right season for docking horses' tails, one is astonished at the torrent of energy and organization that runs to waste in this way. The crushing weight of this apparatus may be guessed from the continuous call for electricians, typists, carrier-pigeon tenders, entertainers, cinema operators, grave-diggers, bath attendants, canteen helpers, cartographists, librarians, and God knows what else. The fighters will become ever fewer and these people ever more numerous—that seems to be quite inevitable, and in this way is built up a grotesque medley of war and peace.

Every genuine soldier is bound to find trench warfare thoroughly repellent. It haunts him with its dead weight. The essential thing is lost sight of among the hosts of things that are ' also necessary ' and ' also important.' No great success can be wrung from it. No great blunders made. For, as in bad housekeeping, the most pressing needs are met while others rise in their place. And then comes the soulless and numerical notion of material superiority, the wearing down of the weaker, to put all else in the background. Thus trench warfare proceeds at last to arithmetic and at such a cost that even the victor may succumb. Hence even in defeat it should be regarded merely as a breathing space, like the clinch in boxing, an interlocking of forces that collect themselves for the next blow.

I regard it in any case as an isolated phenomenon whose date will soon have passed for good, even if it were not already apparent that the theory of mobile war was gaining the upper hand and soon to be seen in action.

With this arises the question of the further development of war. In the correct answer to this question lies the destiny of every nation that has not renounced the task of playing its part in the world. The evolution of war follows a line that is interrupted by longer or shorter intervals of peace. In any review of it, therefore, there are only broken lengths at our disposal and only deductions can be made. The fate of battles depends on the degree to which these deductions approach the actual facts, and this in turn depends on the powers of mind brought to the task. If the form of a new war were dictated by the form in which the last one ended there would be a hiatus at the outset ; for circumstances have altered, even though the alteration has not been confirmed by experience. Civilization is always on the march, and with it its possibilities of expression—among which, naturally, is to be reckoned the prevailing mode of war ; always supposing that by civilization one does not mean the bloodless and anaemic affair of which we are happy to leave the literary and pacific gentlemen in sole possession. If they had their way, we should find our great cities in the hands of Tartars and Cossacks the day after

What this war emphasizes again and again as the new and decisive factor is the entry of the machine into battle and the corresponding retirement of purely manual work. Of our three main arms, to which aviation was added as a fourth, two, infantry and cavalry, if we except the machine-gun companies of the infantry, were wholly occupied in what I call manual work in distinction from machine work. Of these two, the cavalry will soon disappear altogether from the field of battle ; indeed it has disappeared already, even though one cannot accept trench warfare as the normal state of affairs—one that, on the other hand, has given a preponderance to artillery still far short of what is due to it, great as it is already. Perhaps if we had had enough horses the cavalry might in those few hours —when strategic communications between the English and the French were broken through in the great offensive—have taken leave of the battlefield with a last brilliant and historic achievement. As for the future, at any rate, their part is over, even though their mounted artillery and machine-gun companies might be strengthened.

The infantry will, perhaps, hold out longer ; but it, too, is threatened by a process of disintegration that has begun already. The time will come when the single unprotected rifleman will be ground between the mill-stones of machinery. At present, owing again to the influence of trench warfare, this process gives the impression of deterioration. The infantry is burdened with a profusion of weapons by which its weight of fire is increased at the cost of weakening its impetus. Its power of cohesion, too, already endangered by the immense extension of the battlefield, seems to be called in question by the variety of arms. Hence we shall have to break away from the idea of the massed attack in its old form—so inherent particularly in the German blood—that launched the living force of the bayonet by an impulse of its own upon the enemy. It is a question no longer of launching men in mass, but machines—that is to say, death in a concentrated form that only yesterday put at our disposal.

And another prospect too may be foreseen and foretold without losing oneself in the fantasies of a Jules Verne romance ; namely, that these machines will less and less, as ordinarily happens to-day, be conveyed to the points where they are to be put into action, by man- or horse-power. That would belong no longer to an age when men grow up in their homes with motor-cars on every side. The solid earth, in default of roads, and with its changing contours, presents greater difficulties to the passage of machines than do the air and the sea, where the machine has finally established itself in the picture of war. But the peace-time invention of the motor-plough and the war-time one of the tank have made the first steps in overcoming these difficulties.

In imagining the war of to-morrow, war at sea is the first guide ; for it is fought out on a more adaptable element where the mechanical problem came long ago and decisively to the front. A modern battleship gives the fullest expression of the power of a civilized nation. All that the science of mechanism can effect in gunnery, armour, and mobility is combined in it. It is not a question of the power but the will before similar moving fortresses make their appearance in battles on land. On the one hand, machinery insists on centralization ; on the other, tactics demand a distribution in small units that offer little target and are connected only by the object to be achieved.   In a sea-battle, where the factor of carrying capacity plays a greater rôle than with us, it has been found that a big vessel is better than three small ones, whereas on land, where either side could very quickly build heavy batteries, it will perhaps be seen that, on the contrary, three small mechanisms are better than one big one.

It will assuredly be proved that the machine is more powerful than muscle ; and never was a more ruinous object-lesson of this than goes on even to-day, while the ' spirit of the troops ' is thrown into the scale against the mechanism of war.   This is the same fallacy that in another cause leads the pacifists to talk of the battle with spiritual weapons, a fallacy that consists in relating two terms that have no relation to each other.

To talk in this matter of the spirit of the troops merely means the policy of sending them insufficiently equipped against fire-spitting monsters who will blow them to bits like a herd of fallow deer—one of the most tragic spectacles there can be.   The superiority of the spirit—in this context, of the warlike spirit of courage and discipline—can only emerge when it has means that are worthy of it at its command.   It is a matter for the intelligence, perseverance, and inventiveness of a nation to create these means in face of any difficulties and to perfect them to the last detail.

Another speculation is what this arm, that will supersede the infantry as we have so far known it, will be like. Soldiers must give the answer so far as concerns its being, and the mechanic so far as concerns its form. For the first, it turns on mobility, effective fire, and protection ; for the second, on propulsion, automatic fire, armament. To these must be added changing requirements such as noiselessness, camouflage, protection against gas, wireless communications, and a hundred more.

In short, it is a question of creating a machine simple, practical, and well thought out, capable of the utmost and without flourishes, such as could be put into battle as confidently as a motor-car firm sends its best racing car to an international road trial. The comparison with the tank of to-day can be made only in the same sense as the internal-combustion motor car of 1914 may be compared with that of 1900. None the less, the tank is the most important invention of a war rich in contrivances, though it will not perhaps in this war reach by a long way its final stage. It solves a problem that has occupied the minds of all fighting people since the earliest ages in a simple and modern fashion. Mobility, fire, and cover are combined in it, as in the war elephants of the Diadochi, and the testudo of the Roman legion. For this reason and others too, in its further development it is bound to be the decisive engine of the battle of to-morrow with all other arms as its mere accompaniment. Thus it may be taken as certain that even the next war will be fought out in the brief and furious form that answers to the pace of a machine.

Beyond this it may be expected that the idea of mobility will reach the acme to which it is ever moving, in a fusion of the flying squadron and the infantry—in the shape indeed of a flying tank. This will be a heavy, low-flying machine adequately armoured against infantry fire, and designed only for the battle on the ground, while its capacity for flight will serve to bring it forward into action. It will land, join in the fight as a light-armoured car driven by a propeller, and take off again in case of heavy artillery fire, to play its part at other critical points. The idea is not far-fetched though it has never yet been mentioned ; and perhaps the armoured battle-planes, that even to-day fly low over the heads of attacking troops to join for a second or two in the attack, are the first step towards its development.

As mobility increases, the exaggerated importance of artillery will fall away, and it will be made clear that its importance cannot continue to consist in building walls. In the same way the great expectations associated with the use of gas are exploded even by the experiences of trench warfare. To gas even a small area successfully requires so much time and preparation that it is out of the question except when the enemy is entrenched in his position. There remains the transport of gas by aeroplane into the back areas, an operation so troublesome and risky that it can only pay on rare occasions. It is a matter, too, of secondary importance, dependent on the far more important one of superiority in the air ; and it need not be feared that a war will ever turn simply on the stupid release of clouds of gas. Gas will always remain an uncertain factor, dependent on many circumstances ; a resource subjected to all the chances and changes of improvisation on which no reckoning can be made, though at favourable moments it may take an enemy by surprise.

On the other hand, however surprising it may seem in this connection, sheer mass, whether of men or material, will have very little influence on the outcome of a war such as we are considering. In order to understand this, one must have a clear conception of the nature of machinery. It is an expression of the human will to master matter. We see every day in all branches of industry how a new miracle of mind fused into steel abolishes at a stroke all that has gone before. There is no pause. All is movement, pushing relentlessly and madly forward.

Why should it be otherwise in war ? No, an army, too, in its entirety, is more than ever before a machine in which cog grips cog and every ounce of energy is transmitted to the driving belt of the attack—a machine that the will of one man can set in motion. To assemble immense energy in a small space and with it to conquer distance—such is the expression of our will to power. For this an instrument is required so highly polished and fraught with spirit that the notion of mass is utterly foreign to it. The task is to weld the pick of human and mechanical energy into one whole of such tempered force that it will be able to withstand any shock and drive any assault home. Such a task will require time.

This brings us back to the comparison with a battle at sea. When a fleet is proved inadequate in a battle of to-day and its ships are blown up and admirals, captains, officers, engineers, stokers, the men at the torpedoes and guns, and the wireless operators are

drowned, it is all over for this one war, since an instrument of power such as that cannot easily be replaced.
It would hardly occur to a nation to build quickly a
fleet of wooden ships and to man them with men who
had had six weeks' training—in the hope of making
good by numbers what was lacking in quality.

Hence it is easy to see why in this war the fleets,
which, as I said, are the nearest approach to the battle
engine I have been describing, are so carefully husbanded. Each side quails from a decision which
under such advanced conditions of technical perfection
would be final and irremediable.

In the future the same will be true of war on land,
and only inevitable necessity will induce a country to
throw such a product of the miracles of science as a
modern army into the glowing cauldron of battle. An
army like that will be a treasury of resources that
require years to create. One cannot be too emphatic
in asserting that the resolute will is seen in forging the
weapon, and not in hurling those who wield it to
destruction, to run amok like dancers of Dionysus.
There is no denying that battles are won by the feelings,
but the reason must provide the weapons ; otherwise
feelings will shatter themselves against material force.

A danger that must never be lost sight of in the
mechanization of war into which, whether we like it or
not, we are bound to be drawn is the specialization
inseparable from it. The craftsman can quickly adapt
himself to changing needs ; a machine, on the other
hand, is constructed for one defined aim.

We find in fossil-bearing strata of the earth the
remains of beings with powerful armour, claws, and

teeth, which suggest such alarming powers of attack and defence that it is difficult to understand how they allowed themselves to be crowded out in the struggle for life. It can only be supposed that they were specialized to excess in one direction, so that the least alteration in their existence, that is to say, in the fight for existence, sufficed to exterminate them.

This danger of wrong adaptation, of the inability to grip the cogs, is a continual threat to the army of the future, however delicately adjusted to its aim. These gigantic beasts had always this advantage over us—that their circumstances in all probability altered very slowly. An army, on the other hand, passes at a step from the theory and the uncertain make-believe of peace-time manœuvres into the relentless arena of fact. For as actually occurs in a naval battle, the encounter between two air or tank squadrons will be a fight to a finish, and only a rough estimate can be made in peace time of the forces that will turn the scale. That can only be known when it comes to the real thing.

It is scarcely to be expected that European nations whose civilization proceeds from one mighty source will encounter one another with radically different methods of war, as in the case, for example, of the Spaniards and the Aztecs. But there will, all the same, be ideas in the air, such as the automatic steering of aeroplanes or wireless telephony, that one side will develop more quickly and thoroughly than the other. And it can never be foreseen what surprises of a deadly nature may be expected. Even the most perfect espionage is no protection. It is precisely in a short war that such surprises are the more dangerous because there is no time to imitate them or to devise the means of countering them.

This gives another reason against the insane and crushing accumulation of armaments. With the invention of the first iron-plated ship all armadas of wooden ships became valueless ; and the same is true in any sphere of war. What is to-day the highest and the best may be scrap-iron to-morrow. This is where a prospect opens for the weaker side. After a very brief period of naval preparation we were able to engage at the Skagerrack a fleet with a tradition of hundreds of years.

From this it may be seen at once what is the most important quality a nation must possess when its position in the world compels it to reckon with the waging of great wars. This quality is more than ever, in peace as well as in war, the proof of its fitness to survive. It is the capacity for the speedy development of a large programme. Even this war differs from all previous ones in that it is not fought out on one fixed plan. New problems extort fresh spasmodic exertions. Programme after programme, whether justified or exploded by the event, clothes its protean form. The result is a test of endurance that taxes every section and every resource of the nations involved. The grip and organizing power of industry, the industry of the masses, the national basis of finance, the superiority in science and its relation to practical needs, the development of communications, the general level of education—who can enumerate all that is laid under contribution ? First and foremost, however, it is a question whether it is rooted with every fibre in the present day.

But where does the common man come in in all this ?
Is not all this a soulless and crushing business ?   A
cold exalting of mechanical forces, an array of formulae
in physics, chemistry, and the higher mathematics ?
Is this to be the test of life ?   Is it not giving the
intellect and big business the mastery of the earth ?
Is the brain on its technical side the best we have
to offer ?

This is the question put now and then by the
cultured German who prizes Weimar above Essen, and
by the soldier too when he sees the instincts of the hero
subdued to the technique of war.   This is the opinion
of the generation that still believes it to be a superior
person's duty to turn his back on mechanism as the
enemy of the spirit.

But what do we, the coming generation, care for all
this ?   To us, too, the machine is something external,
something that we have set up out of ourselves. ·But
it is our indispensable resource, whether in peace or
war ; and for that reason we endorse and accept it.
Every civilization has been great in creations that can
be set beside our own, but the machine is what we
ourselves have created and we have a right to be proud
of it.   Certainly, it is only an instrument, but one that
witnesses to our strength of will.   As we rise with its
help to the height of our achievements in all other
spheres of reality, so we must in war too.   We defend
ourselves with its help and we attack with it.   And is it
not we ourselves who stand behind it ?   Is it not our
life and our blood that provide its impulse ?   The
sword is only the prolongation of the arm—but only so
long as it is wielded.   And so the machine, too, is only

enhanced power—but only so long as we ourselves are powerful. The moment we give in, no machine in the world can help us. But as long as we do not lose the feeling that calls out to every valiant man, ' You are born to rule,' we shall always know how to create the best instruments of power of our time.

Good equipment is prized only by people whose virile nerve is still vigorous. Is there any danger that the individual fighter will not match in strength of character what is gained in the effectiveness of his mechanism ? No one could say so who has been through the war with open eyes. Even the man who to-day controls so primitive an instrument as the machine-gun shows up to advantage from the rest. Whether it is that he is a picked man or that he has grown to meet an increased responsibility, I have scarcely seen one who did not stand to his gun like a man. Any one could bear me out in this. I have noticed in these men the keen pleasure of shooting at a target with their weapons. I am fond of shooting myself and have made good practice with every sort of fire-arm, but nothing pleases me more than seeing the bullets of a machine-gun plastering the target in front of me. How a man becomes one with his machine is shown in a small way by the skilled machine-gunner, who can shoot his signature on a bank of earth, and gets to the point of aiming no longer by the bead and notch or using the telescopic sight, since he prefers to follow with his naked eye above the rattling machine the spurting dust of the bullets as they strike, and thus to get the best results in the quickest, surest, and simplest way. This is a method not provided for in any regula-

tions.   This instinctive technique must be even more
inherent in the blood of the air-scout who has to shoot
with his whole machine—a winged machine-gun in
fact—or to fasten upon his prey like a swallow upon a
flitting insect.   Thus we can see that the mechanics of
war not only mean increased power but also make the
highest demands on the men concerned.   The best
men will have the best machinery and the best
machinery must have the best men—for the two are
inseparable.

THE weather has cleared and the rain has driven the sultry air out of the trenches. We have had another proof to-day how careful and attentive to every detail one has to be. A runner was shot through the back of the head as he was coming along the trench that connects the dugout with the front line. Up to now there has never been a casualty in this bit of trench ; and the only explanation is that the rain has washed away the banked-up earth on the sides and in this way exposed the trench to the enemy's view at a place where it runs slightly downhill. It is always the same : one gets used to danger, as the hands do in a powder factory, and at last careless of it. Now we have laid a row of poles across the trench with wire-netting and grass on top and so masked the place from view.

A horse was hit last night near Puisieux Alley. It was harnessed to a waggon loaded with trench-mortar ammunition, destined for the hedge-trench where there is a heavy trench-mortar emplacement for firing to the front of Copse 125. In earlier days when a horse was shot it lay where it fell, rotted, and poisoned the whole neighbourhood till somebody threw a sack of quicklime on it. To-day it is as though we were in the tropics where vultures are at home. At first great pieces disappear from the hams and shoulders, and within the day nearly all the flesh is removed from the bones. It finds its way into the dixies and makes a powerful brew.   So it was to-day.   H., like a regular freebooter, was one of the first to hear of this windfall and brought the tongue along.   We found it excellent.

We live just as though in a beleaguered fortress. The English have even asserted in their newspapers that we submit human bodies to a chemical process in order to turn them to account.   We have rebutted the charge with great earnestness.   Perhaps it would have been more impressive if we had said : ' Certainly, we barbarians are glad even after our deaths to be hurled at your heads in the form of nitro-glycerine.'

' Mark this,' said General Rapp, when he answered the summons to surrender Strasburg, ' I will not surrender the place till my soldiers have to eat human flesh, as those in my command in Dantzig did with the hindquarters of the Russians.'

THE two days in the main support line have passed none too well. They began happily and ended sadly.

On the first day mulled wine was sent up with the rations. In some village behind a large stock of wine was discovered in a purposely inundated cellar, and the proceeds were divided out among the troops. The brew followed the rule ' not often but plenty,' a rule that our view of life endorses ; and I was able to send a runner forward with a dixie of it so that B. might have a carousal. I knew that it would be welcome, for at midday we had seen hit after hit among the bare trees, though it was quiet elsewhere ; and the Verey lights eddied up into the air, calling for a reply from our artillery and sinking again in twin green stars. Now and then a runner or a stretcher had crossed our trench, and though we sat at peace in the midday sunshine we had a feeling that something was wrong. At night, however, the fire slackened off and we could get down to our mulled wine. It was made apparently of the best white Bordeaux fortified with plum-brandy by a well-meaning cook who thought more of its strength than its taste. We were reminded of sumptuous days in Champagne when we slept on unthreshed sheaves and acquired at twenty years old a palate for wine that our grandfathers might have envied us. The evening, at any rate, passed very cheerfully, and S. and D. made their appearance and sat carousing with unbuttoned tunics.

It is a fact that the best place for drinking is just in front of the enemy.   After the war I shall have a dugout sunk beneath the cellar at home, just as Robinson Crusoe built himself a hut when he got back to his native town so that he and Friday could remember their island.   It will have to be quite unadorned ; roof, floor, and walls of planks ; a bunk and a bench and a table of inch-thick dugout boarding.   Against the wall there will be a narrow shelf with the boxes of Verey-light cartridges on it, a steel helmet, and a rifle hanging beneath it by its strap.   There will be a candle stuck in a Burgundy bottle, and in a corner a little iron stove with the heavy bayonet lying beside it for splitting wood.   No one shall enter it but genuine front-line fellows who know that it is the right thing to knock their pipes out on the table, to spit on the floor, and to put no rein on the tongue.   We shall drink from enamelled mugs and mess-tins, put on our old torn and shot-riddled tunics, and wear no decorations on them, needless to say.   There will be no lack, doubt-less, of top-hatted occasions when we shall listen to long speeches.   It will not be there, however, but in this retreat of mine, that I shall recall those times that were more to me than all the rest of my life.   Of course there will have to be those other occasions, but not for us.   There will be plenty of others to put in an appearance at those official ceremonies.

More—I feel sure that we shall do well to oppose our own deep and vital emotion to this official patriotism. The experience we have been through will, I believe, knit up again many severed threads.   We need the resolute virile strength that goes without saying and is expressed quietly and without gestures. Not too many decorations, not too much uniform, but more of that unemphatic attitude that goes without saying. Above all, a realization that our country is like the air that we all breathe. No one must put himself forward as one supremely called. There are things of which a man speaks little. They lie too deep to jump to his tongue. Such are the concerns of love and belief, and those of our country must again be one. Its roots must go once more so deep that they reach our bottommost strength. We need poets again like Eichendorff and Schenkendorf, and a state of feeling such as must have inspired the poem ' Coming down the Rhine.' We must carry on what many of the young people in Germany had begun before the war, inspired by an unconscious impulse, but by a strength of their own—I mean those holiday expeditions into the country in small bands of friends. When you stand at early morning on a mountain top with the smoke of the village curling up far below in a song of busy life, or when you loiter in old towns that bow beneath their weight of history, or when, finally, you look with open eyes on the rich art collections and the might of industry in great cities, you need no one to tell you what your country means. You feel then that the whole world is beautiful and that your own country has a beauty of its own. Such a feeling is not inspired by literary or military or social flourishes. We must drink where the spring is freshest and purest. Then we shall have the root of the matter within us—a deep emotion ; and the form will come of itself.

Form is not in reality so important as it has often

been made with us. The exaggerating of it betrays an uncertainty quite opposed to a racial and native strength. This over-emphasis of form has often had injurious and ludicrous results. I have known quite sensible fellows who, when they put on a uniform, a decoration, or even a frock-coat for a ceremonial occasion, looked suddenly as though their limbs were screwed into their bodies in a strange and artificial manner. This is nauseating and such people must be made to understand that patriotism is not intended for giving them an air. But as long as the academic, the military, and many other dark places of our life are not cleared up, the real strength of our people can never be made one. I do not mean by this the justifiable pride a man has in his profession, but that offensive aloofness that withdraws him from his fellows in other walks of life. That is the real social question. It is not a question of money but of feeling.

These gentlemen were put to shame when at the outbreak of the war the whole nation, as every one knows, thronged with one accord to the colours ; and indeed no one who looks back to that time without a feeling of gratitude and religious prostration is a German. That moment made us realize that we were, in the truest and highest sense, all alike, however unlike in rank and possessions. The whole nation was shot through by the single feeling of being one race, one in flesh and blood, one in the consciousness of presenting an undivided front to the outer world. I remember, too, many occasions just before an attack, when I felt this feeling of brotherhood, of an inner bond, with which not every time is favoured. We must keep it in times of peace as well. That is one of the duties that our generation alone can perform, and the work will fall chiefly on the younger and better educated. A new and strong and sound national feeling must be created among us by rigorous self-discipline and conveyed to the mass of the people by every means, even by those of the Salvation Army. We shall see that a comradeship between students and working-men need not only have a revolutionary aim as it had in Russia. It is clear that such an alliance will renew an intensity of feeling that can only be looked for as an after-effect of this war ; and once it is established all petty grievances will fall away at a blow. When that is so, we shall be able to address our country in the words of Hölderlin : ' And do not count the dead ! For you, our country, not a man too many falls.'

But now for the daily life again. We shall not be blamed for taking life by the forelock when we can and while we are in the trough of the waves between one danger and the next. Our pleasures are few enough. Indeed there is only one—to drink now and then and to be jolly together. Every time may be the last, and hence we enjoy it as wildly as if it were. That is why I said that drinking is at its best in face of the enemy. One clutches at life here in any shape, to squeeze from it what one can, and the blood circles in the veins quicker and more joyfully than it ever does elsewhere. Debauch for us is one of the things we ask of life, and it does us good when the reply comes fast and furious. Perhaps one does the staff an injustice, for in the main it is certainly we who give them the example, and one

of which we are not ashamed.   For as long as there is
song and laughter and exuberant spirits, we know that
we still have it in us ; and many a one has passed
straight from such moments to his death after spend-
ing at least one night of glamour just before.   To-day,
too, compared with previous wars, we die with little
ceremony and alone.   Hence it means something to
show beforehand in an hour of enthusiasm that air in
the face of death that the brave man used to exhibit in
the ranks in times gone by.

   This is why I hope that the poor fellow who met a
sudden death in the midst of us this morning was able
yesterday to enjoy a few moments that took him out of
these relentless surroundings.   The morning was very
quiet but for a few isolated shells that fell in the village
and in the copse ; and whether it was that there was a
mistake of aim on the other side, or whether the powder
in the shell was damp or the charge carelessly weighed,
I cannot say, but in any case there came a direct hit on
the spot where Puisieux Alley crosses the main support
line, and just at that moment a man was standing in
front of his dugout looking through the barrel of his
rifle after cleaning it.

   I know well these moments when the unexpected
happens.   One is concerned with quite other matters
and the ear seems scarcely to hear the rush of the iron
cylinder that describes its arc above the level ground—
seems, for within there is hidden a truer instinct like a
watchdog on the alert, and it tells one that the shadow
of death broods over the scene and does not let the least
sign of danger go by without raising its warning voice.
We were brought up in such security that at first we

heard this voice indistinctly as a confused though urgent call ; but we have learned to listen for it. We have rediscovered the link with a power that is deeper and stronger than the reason by which we believed we could meet all the demands of life, and which, all the same, leaves us in the lurch just when life and death are at stake.

For when all of a sudden the long-drawn howl, high up in the air and scarcely noticeable at first, passes into a clearer note, and within us, whatever we may be busied upon, there flashes out the red signal that warns us of death, a few fractions of a second only are left for action. And while reason is at a standstill and leaves us helplessly to our fate, that other—which I should find it ungrateful to call by any threadbare name such as instinct or presence of mind—leaps out like a loyal and trusty animal, throws us behind the nearest ditch or into some hole that we had never seen till that moment and gives our endangered limbs a spasm of energy that otherwise would have been quite beyond us.

When, long after, reason comes on the scene to see what was best to be done, it has to admit that even the most precise calculation could not have made a better and surer valuation of time and space. And further, in utterly unforeseen circumstances, this trusty watcher makes at least a pathetic effort in our defence. Doctors say that a soldier has scarcely ever been hit through the open eye. In almost every case the closed lid was first pierced. Thus we find for ourselves a hidden meaning in these incalculable times, and we shall occupy ourselves less and less with seeking in this relation for causes and connections. On every side we are brought by this war into touch with the miraculous. We have a glimpse of a driving force beneath the conscious life, a mighty will ; and we consent to surrender ourselves to it. It is only on looking back, as in the little instance I mentioned, that the reason sees how near destruction was, and then talks ungratefully, unbelievingly, and short-sightedly of luck or accident.

There is even more in these moments that flash out like lightning and almost outstrip time—when the blinding rays of death rend the veil that lies over our senses. There comes a point when life, after forcing the body to a last terrified and spasmodic energy, sees no way out. And at this point terror vanishes, for it has no purpose left. That does not happen, though, till the body has been hit ; for till then life does not give up ; it still reckons with misfires, duds, wounds, and all sorts of remote possibilities. But after that it lets the arms sink ; it has done the duty prescribed it by mysterious laws and now looks death full in the face. I have felt this myself. I do not pride myself on it, for it is the same with every one and perhaps I ought to say, it has happened to me. It is an experience not easy to describe—a feeling as though one passed out of a storm into a still haven. One surrenders gladly to what before seemed too horrible. I remember the peculiar half-jesting, half-consolatory thought : ' Is this all ? ' I am convinced that this moment precedes every death, however weary and bitter the fight for life may have been. And I must say that life combines a fine fighting attitude with deep wisdom. It gives itself up with a smile after it has kept up the battle to the last drop of its blood. Thus it is that the Hero stands for us as a particularly radiant picture of life and one that art and love delight to reverence.

The man who died this morning has all behind him now. If the question is asked whether he, a simple peasant from the Lüneburger Heath, could have the feelings I describe, the answer is that here, thank God, there are no distinctions.

He was the only man out in the trench, where he was standing busied with his rifle. Immediately the shell burst the force of the explosion sent him rolling down the few steps into the dugout where two other men slept. He had a frightful wound in the skull. From the account I had, it must have been a ghastly moment ; for this shattered brain, obeying some automatic impulse, attempted, a few moments before its total extinction, to bring out a verse of a soldier's song.

The news of such events passes very quickly along the trench. I was on the spot five minutes after the disaster. This is one of the most important duties of an officer in command—one that can only be passed over under very great stress of circumstances. For one thing, it is the part of him whose rank makes him the representative of the state to take leave of one who leaves the battlefield for ever ; and also such scenes spread a feeling of depression and listlessness of which no one can form any idea who has not himself experienced it, for it is natural that all who witness them imagine themselves in a like case. This has to be tackled. Orders have to be given so as to have the distraction of activity; and the body must be removed as quickly as possible, for the sight of it will be more than some can bear. It is not right to leave dead bodies on

a fire-step, as often happens, in order to have them
carried back under cover of night.

When I arrived the dead man had been brought up
into the trench again, and his section were standing
round him.   An attempt had been made to bind up the
wound, but the bandages were saturated with blood at
once and the head was a red and shapeless mass.   I
told the stretcher-bearers to remove his identity disc,
paybook, and valuables, and to wrap him in a ground-
sheet.   Soon after, they had gone with their sad load
along Puisieux Alley.

Though the war has gone on a long time and I have
seen hundreds, thousands indeed, of severe casualties,
of mutilated bodies and whole fields of corpses, I have
never got used to these sights.   Every time I have to
make an effort to get over them.   How I succeed in
doing so I cannot say.   It is rather as though I refuse
to focus on what is before me, and fix my eyes on the
distance even while I look on them.   It is the abstrac-
tion of the soldier, not so easy as the doctor's, for the
doctor can see a case before him while the soldier sees
his own case.

It is exactly here that the touchstone of inner forti-
tude is found.   For the effect of such sights is not only
that they touch the nerves.   They raise as well, even
in the simplest mind, questions of a moral import—
questions about the meaning of such occurrences and
the responsibility for them.   Hence the pacifists find
here the point to lay stress on.   Opponents of war
never tire of bringing up its grim and hideous features—
men burnt alive, torn in pieces and mutilated, their
brains spurting out, their viscera hanging out.   It is

only natural that there should be numerous adherents
of an argument based upon the fear of pain, real and
imaginary, and the safety of the body.   And when one
is dismally faced by the dark visage of the war, as we
are to-day, the argument is not easy to rebut.

Pacifism will rise and fall with the times.   A period
of weariness or one that lacks great ideas will always
give it a clear field.   And rightly, for when young men
have no great aim before their eyes, why should they
sacrifice themselves ?   When they have, on the other
hand, they will of their own accord be carried away by
the force that quails at nothing.   The proud and indisputable right of the victor to decide the world's
destiny is so intoxicating a prospect to a race that does
not doubt its call to greatness, that all else must appear
of no account.   In face of this, death, suffering, and
all the horrors that lie on the surface of things fall away,
and it is certain that the greater moral strength resides
in such a conception.   Every materialistic dissuasion
weighs in the opposing scale—to be outweighed by the
hero's ' So be it ' that encircles him with a super-
natural glory.   When all is at stake difficulties are
nothing.

Once more it is Hölderlin who gives clear expression
to all this :

' I would not choose to die for nothing.   But I would
choose to fall for my country on a mound of slain.'

This raises the important question how one is to
impress this on the soldier.   How is one to proof and
temper him for the frightful impressions of modern war
when he crosses the frontier in unsuspecting enthusiasm ?

Our enemies say we took young recruits into the slaughter-houses to accustom them to the sight of blood.   This method would be effective and commendable if the endurance of the horrible were merely a matter of nerve.   But, as I have said, brute force plays a smaller part here than one might think.   Certainly hardness comes in.   A schooling in manly exercise and sport, long marches, endurance of fatigue and privation, and the putting up with vexations of every sort, are all of them important.   But they are not the essential.   We have often seen weak nervous natures, men of little muscle and refined faces, who were capable of bearing a strain in a way that could not be explained by their bodily strength.

A generation worthy to represent its country in battle is not to be fashioned by any method : it springs from the primitive vigour of the people, and all the educational means by which these young men might seem to be brought up proceed from the same source as the nation has to thank for the possessing of these young men at all.   It is easy to demand that historical associations shall be evoked in school and university, but what help are all the great ideas of the past if they do not fall on ears and hearts that feel themselves called to do the like ?   It is easy to say, too, that art must kindle a national consciousness, but if there is not in any case a depth of conviction, the only result is war memorials of plaster and boring historical pictures. The same is true of the family, of society, of the army, of philosophy, and anything by means of which men may be influenced.   None of them can create ideas for which a man will die.   They can represent these ideas and enforce them, give them expression, or carry them on further.   But where there is not a disposition of the soul ready, they grip on air.

This disposition, however, is of a religious nature, and the outer symbol that draws it forth is—sacrifice. Hence it is a religious question that comes to birth in a soldier who stands before a town laid in ruins or a comrade's mutilated body.   He asks himself : ' Is the highest that I believe and fight for worth this sacrifice ? ' And the answer he gives, whether he knows it or not, decides whether his courage can get the better of these impressions and this onslaught of material, or whether he quails before them.   He says to himself either that it is senseless or that it cannot be helped ; and this feeling of an inner necessity will confirm him in a resolute bearing.   This is the real 'moral factor' that tolerates no interference and by which battles are won, because the strength of conviction in an idea and the willingness for sacrifice in those who fight for it finds in this moral factor its direct expression.   Where the love of country is grounded in the heart there can be no gainsaying it.   The resources of the State will stand behind it, as the Church is behind faith ; and art will flourish like the art of the medieval masters who could represent the sufferings of the martyrs with a boundless ardour.   Then young men will find the greatest honour in the hardest tasks and nothing will have power to shake them.

In such a land the love of peace will be honoured, but pacifism—never.

WE were badly shelled with shrapnel during the relief and had two casualties. We were fagged out, but all the same the first night was devoted to drinking. It was comic when towards morning there was a false alarm of gas owing to a few shells whose fumes were certainly rather odd, and we suddenly found ourselves sitting round the table with our masks on, like a circle of sea-spectres with goggle eyes and fantastic beaks.

On the second morning I had to take part in a parade, a comedy for which I have little use. I have always been careful not to say so ; but the march past in a set style that recalls late baroque and seems even more unnatural out here, because there is little time for practising it, always makes a painful impression on me. I pride myself on being easily enthusiastic, but on these occasions even I cannot rouse my feelings to the required pitch. I am always glad when this business of marching past the inspecting officer in parade step, like a puppet drawn by a thread in its nose, is over. Here, as in many other of the formal parts of our military make-up, is to be seen the oriental element of Prussianism.

We have much to thank Prussianism for, but a great deal of its outward show needs severe curtailment. Incidentally, I have made the significant observation that Saxon border regiments, among which there is much Wendish blood, are more Prussian than the Prussians.

The parade march has accompanied us faithfully throughout the whole war, and I am convinced that with peace it will enter on new glories. I am not going to speak of those survivors of the war who will stream back to their units from the shelter of safe jobs and try to carry on again from the point where we put ourselves on mobilization ; for in any case there is about us a regimental sticklishness, a savour of red tape and an ardour for the traditional routine that can only be explained by saying that we arrived so lately as a world-power. In many respects we have remained pro-vincials, quill-drivers, gendarmes, and paymasters who have not grown to meet the new resources which have made them rich overnight. All honour to the virtues of old Prussia, but not to its fossilized punctilio. A little more of Hamburg might well have been erected on those foundations. A war for world-power requires other measures than a war for a province or two. There is no denying that there is a touch of dryness and prosaicness in Prussianism that, once its genius, is now its habit only—a lack of imagination that the younger generation too easily, though with a sound instinct, find chilling. Hence, too, the half-bottle of champagne that Bismarck said the Prussian needed.

This system offers too little room precisely for the best elements—for the voluntary enlistments which unquestionably were superior to all the rest. Again and again we had to wonder whether we were reading the books of von Peter or the memoirs of the old Nettlebeck, who was certainly one of the best Prussians, however many there may be, and certainly are to-day, to scout this assertion with indignation.

But there is no need of books. One has only to appeal to the spirit in which we were received when we hastened in our hundreds and thousands to the barracks. It was the scurviest imaginable, and the first expression of it was the slow march. It often seemed that the first essential was to purge us of enthusiasm, as though it were a most unmilitary feeling and opposed to discipline. I was then eighteen years old, but I was not too uncritical to think to myself : ' To the devil with a war that begins with the slow march.'

It is so easy, after all, to keep a body of young and enthusiastic troops in good-going form. We were ready and eager for physical exertion and to submit to rigorous training ; but we wanted war, iron war—not the orderly room. It was an obvious joke to christen us 'the volunteers,' but it was a sign too that we were actually regarded as outsiders. I do not mind saying that I consider the spirit of such an army as the young Napoleon led to Italy and Egypt as the best there can be. There is always more to thank the enemy for than one thinks, and so it is between us and that great man of Europe.

We young Germans would be the last to reject Prussianism so far as its moral side goes. We know well that the inspired and practical founders of it had an unsurpassed wisdom in setting men to a job. They built up a machine that worked economically, exactly, and reliably, and one that could inspire enthusiasm in spite of its bleak outlines, because its aim was not self but the greatness of the country. It was designed to last—which explains the elimination of the personal element ; for a system reared on personality must fall with it too.   Here neither the greatest nor the smallest was indispensable.   He did not dare to be.   From the death sentence which was said to have been passed on the Crown Prince Frederick, to the fall of Steinmetz, and right on into this war, generation after generation was reinforced by this will of steel.   We are still trained on this iron system of bend or break, and let us hope that we shall never lose the curt formula, ' Company is under my command,' with which the survivor takes over without delay the duties of the fallen.

It has been shown, however, that the machine-made State cannot for ever be kept going by the *perpetuum mobile* of an idea.   In course of time it loses force. Then it must either fall under the sway of a personality like Bismarck, or else be eaten out by its unceasing and punctual routine.

And thus it is with the march past.   Undoubtedly it incorporates the highest pitch of order and discipline, and a glamour of heroism, too, finds its fitting expression in the rattle of arms and in that specially Prussian march step.   But it is no longer in tune with our time, nor with an army composed as ours is, nor with the resources that decide a battle of to-day.   It may be argued that the march past gives the simplified and traditional picture of battle ; but in my opinion the important matter is the link with the present and the symbolizing of the battles of to-day.   Even the man in the ranks has a fine sense of this.

In itself the march past is as necessary now as ever

it was.   Now, even more than ever, officers and men, often widely separated during battle, must be given the opportunity to see each other face to face.   There must be some means, too, of inspiring each individual with a feeling of solidarity with large numbers of troops, a feeling often lost in widely extended battle-fronts ; and commanding officers must be able to judge of the spirit of the troops they are to put into the line.   This, however, for example, is one thing that the icy cere- mony of the formal parade entirely defeats ; for the officer can only form an opinion of the standard of drill, and this to-day has no longer any decisive importance. If one considers a review of Macedonians under Alexander, of the Old Guard under Napoleon, one realizes that other means could be thought of to suit present conditions.

Further, parade before an engagement should make the rhythm of battle a living thing and afterwards replace it by the classic triumphal procession as a prelude to the final and victorious return home. Lastly, in peace time it must exalt the idea of war and break in upon the periods of training as a ceremony, but not one to make the whole regiment, from the major to the youngest recruit, sweat blood for four weeks beforehand.

It is not difficult to form a picture of the parade of the future.   Think of the mighty concentration that preceded our battles—the motor-hauled batteries, the tanks and heavy trench-mortars that rolled forward, interrupted by troops in storm equipment, by search- lights, machine-gun sections, signallers — think, in short, of all that immense apparatus that answers to the resources of to-day. It is this that makes the more powerful appeal to our feelings. We feel ourselves then at the acme of the warfare of our day—of a time such as that when the streets of Rome rang beneath the Tripudium of the legions, or when the conqueror of Asia passed in review the phalanxes, the elephants, the sickle-chariots, and the wheeled fortresses with which he laid in ruins the cities of the Tyrrhenian Sea.

This is the feeling our parades must evoke. It will not be difficult to array the power we dispose of to-day in an impressive spectacle. A parade such as this will differ as much from those of the present day as the spiked leather helmet from the steel helmet, and as the bright uniform from the simple field-grey tunic. It will find its place in a time when we are beginning to feel the beauty of machinery, and it will have something of that beauty in which there are no superfluous flourishes.

Here is the line of severance between the spirits of two ages, and already to-day one can feel in the army two entirely contradictory influences.

WHEN it is too hot at midday in my dugout, I unbutton my uniform and go for a walk with a blanket over my arm to find a place for a sun-bath. This is one of the advantages of a countryside without women. On the other hand, there is always discipline, and I have to avoid meeting men of my company in case they might not feel equal to seeing me practising the Simple Life.

To-day I selected a clearing among the birches with which the embankment is overgrown, and read a book that I have often read before and will often read again if I live to do so. It was *My Brown Book* by Hermann Löns, the man who has given the best picture of my native country. It is only by reading a book like this that one feels the link with the soil. But there is another reason for the attraction Löns has for me. He is not only related to me in race, but as a comrade too, for he fell in the autumn of 1914 in the first wave of the war enthusiasm, and he belonged to this regiment, which consists almost entirely of Lower Saxons, and to a company of which I was later in command. He was killed by a bullet in an infantry engagement, and he was one who knew how to value such a death. He was one of the finest of men, and so death came easily to him. I have spoken to some of those who were near him on the night when he was hit, rifle in hand, behind a heap of stones.

If I were asked who Löns was, I should find it hard

to answer. Beneath a simplicity that makes the same effect as water after all other drinks, he conceals deeper complexities that are expressed in the destiny of his life as well as in many of his books. But the essential thing in him is his German core, and this gave him at last the ascendance over the troubles of his time and of his own life.

Löns stands apart from his day as an artist, and hence in literary circles he has had small recognition. We shall always look back with pride on the years before the war when Germany made herself felt abroad, when she built ships, constructed railways in Asia, founded colonies and coaling stations, while a mighty army backed aims that were always pushed further and more courageously forward. It was a time of growth in which much was achieved, and it is only natural that in its haste all the resources of it were not developed to an equal extent. Perhaps it is inevitable that outward expansion means inward loss. Perhaps the moments of a nation's whole and equal development represent a rare and passing stroke of fortune, when many lines of its evolution meet in one point and then branch out once more at divergent angles.

It cannot be denied that there was little in contemporary art for us young Germans. It was not our privilege to find the very age with which we felt we had grown up and were identified reflected in the work of master spirits. It was cast in our teeth that we found machines more perfect than pictures, dramas, or novels, and that we gave ourselves up more and more to the study of mechanics and natural science. True—but what were we offered in the years when our souls felt that first hunger on whose satisfaction the whole of after-life depends ? Who gave us a mould or pointed out a lofty aim to which we should direct our steps ? Did art in the Germany of our day fulfil its duty towards us ? Or were we perhaps people whom no enthusiasm for greatness or beauty can touch ?

We have proved since then, by the only proof there is of anything, that this was not the case with us, and that a thirst for enthusiasm burned in us as ardently as any that can be conceived. When the call came, lecture-rooms, schools, counters, workshops, factories were emptied. There was a call here that demanded the surrender and sacrifice of the whole man—and this is what young men desire. Hence an intoxication took possession of us in these days. It released us from a life in which the deeper aims were lacking.

For the transformation that overtook us in a night—into men who, though they did not know perhaps all that was at stake, felt it all the same in all its power—we have no one but ourselves to thank and the native land that was in our blood. We had not had a religious education, and whatever may be said against such an education, it has at least the merit of laying a foundation from which the feelings can develop ; neither had the art of our day taken on this task. And since the humanities in the good old sense of the word were being pushed more and more into the background, emphasis was laid almost entirely upon the mind.

In art, too, there was nothing but the mind, blank and icy, and incomplete in its grasp at that. Why bring in names ! It is enough to consider the themes that were dished up for us. Even if we were not very clear about it, we always felt the lack of something there though it might be beyond our expression. Thus it came that if one asked a young German what poet he found himself most in sympathy with, one was certain to be given a name from the far past, or a French, Norse, or Slav one. We were not able to name with pride those two or three who serve to make a school and whose position cannot be challenged. After the war that laid again the foundations of our national unity, we had—with the single exception of Nietzsche, whom we thank for almost all that had power to move us strongly —not one who, like Balzac, ' wished to complete with the pen what the sword had begun.' Even modern Russian art, an art of revolution directed against the state, was at least Russian. The blood of the nation beat in it and made it strong. That is what matters. Art need not be ' patriotic,' for not at all times does the state, as it is for the moment constituted, provide the moving idea ; but it must be national, for it is only from the native soil that anything great and strong can come. It is not worth bothering with anything that could be written equally well in Stockholm, Paris, or Berlin. There must be substance when anything of eternity is to be kneaded in.

On the other hand, we find works whose origin is in a small and defined area and whose importance far exceeds these limits. The universal is reflected in the particular, and this is the feeling Löns gives us. I will not hazard an opinion of his absolute worth. There are no standards to measure him by. In any case he is one of those wry figures who arouse more interest than a healthy man of normal development. Perhaps he has not the refinement of style possessed by those others, but instead he has strength—and it is one of our peculiarities to prize strength more than adroitness. His novels, too, are not of importance, but whatever he writes of the race and of the country has the breath of his large and open nature, and no echo in it of the intellectual chatter of the coteries. There is comprehensiveness instead of disintegration, a clear if limited feeling. He stands on his feet ; and he has a love of his native land and of the people that is as deep as it is simple and unaffected. It is the writing of a man who, whenever he could, escaped from the noise of the big towns, plunged into the solitudes of woods and moors and heaths, and gave himself up to lonely contemplation.

We find in him a love of all that a bleak country offers, a country, compared to others, waste and barren, but his own. Löns finds the right path, which we all ought to keep in mind, from his own outspoken personality to his stock, from his stock to the people. He knows what we should never forget, that the strength of Germany resides in its stocks, and so he tries to steep himself in the atmosphere of his own—the Nether Saxon stock—and to trace out its relation with myth and history and the land in all their ramifications, and this is not a study from outside. It is pursued on the spot. He knows each village and parish. He throws himself upon the bosom of the earth and listens to what it says ; and he finds in sport his great pretext.

Thus we accompany him at early morning when the mist is still on the moor, at noon when the heat glows in the lonely groups of pines among the heather, or in the moist gloaming of a springtime evening when the first snipe are calling and the sense of renewed life stirs strongly in its sleep about the ancient woods. We experience in these solitudes the feelings of men under arms. We are in touch with nature in a manly and untroubled way. But these solitudes are not dead. There is a clamour of voices, a flood of life and a manifestation of power where nothing is great and nothing is small. We pass wonderful hours with a fever of waiting in our blood, lying at length among grasses and undergrowth, where life in a thousand forms creeps about us and dances above us on glazed wings. We feel that we ourselves are some of those minute beings. Trees are gigantic, the grass a forest ; life and death rush more swiftly to encounter us, and happiness becomes a mad and fleeting second between two infinities of which we know nothing ; and we crowd all enjoyments into the little and simple occupations that completely satisfy us.

Everywhere there is antagonism pressed home with sting and tendril, poisoned tooth and claw ; and yet above all is a higher unity, a cosmic power presiding over all the ceaseless motion, and of this every atom in these hours when the earth exhales its intoxicating breath seems to be aware. Thus it seems a pagan joy to press the body to the earth, a pantheistic intoxication which perhaps Walt Whitman alone has put into words.

Löns compels us to share this feeling with him when

the roebuck suddenly leaps to sight in front of us. Sport and the kill have a meaning of their own in these surroundings. We are offering sacrifice to some invisible God of manhood. The gold glancing beast in which a moment ago life was at the full now lies bleeding on the grass, and becomes a symbol that links us with those primitive passions where everything has its source. And at the same time when we see the darkened eyes, the sadness of young Parsifal, who had to shoot at birds and wept when he hit them, comes over us. We realize in those fleeting moments that life can only assert itself in its own destruction. Yet this reflection pales in the sense of pride at having achieved a manly aim by exertion, cunning, patience, and cool blood.

Löns is no wallower in sensation. There is a fresh breeze blowing through all he writes. He speaks, as a matter of course, as a man to men. He stands for all that is primitive and strong ; and whenever it is a question of the country, of race, tradition, and character, he is always at home. He often breaks out in indignation over a time that strives to level everything to a dead uniformity He takes under his wing the rare fauna that are hunted down because of the harm they do, and would like to see them preserved—' because as things are going we shall soon have made the country a desert.' Though a hunter, he is sorry to see the black stork, the raven, the heron, the crane, the otter, and stagbeetle being exterminated as the waste lands and old oak forests gradually disappear, just as the old barrows are blasted to make road metal, and as the potash workings bring strange folk who care nothing for old customs on to the moors.   But again and again he returns with joy to his conviction that the old breed cannot be stamped out.   In the villages with their low roofs and the crossed horse-skulls on their gables a fine tough-fibred race flourishes still.

These are the reasons why we, in whom the experience of war has caused a great stocktaking of values, see in Löns one of the few whom we can accept without reserve.   It is not a question of his greatness.   There may be greater writers, but they follow paths that are ours no longer.   We disown them and their mental agilities shall bluff us no more.   We mean to preserve the link with blood, earth, and feeling.   These are words that have been hammered into us on one side and ridiculed on the other.   Now we are clear about their meaning and shall make no more mistakes.   Here lies the source of the strength we need ; for we have heavy tasks ahead of us.   Löns gives us a first signpost and that is his great service to us.   We shall never forget that of him.

It goes without saying that a man like him was among the first to fly to arms at the outbreak of the war, though he was over military age.   It was a matter of course for one who made manliness the central point of his view of life.   The clean shot that so often brought down his game put an end to him too.   He died in a time after his own heart.   We think as he did when we see this death through a soldier's eyes, one who knows that it is better to fall in battle than to die in bed.   One can die at any time, but opportunities for falling have to be seized.   We shall not forget him any more than we shall forget Gorch Fock who met his end on the North

Sea, or Walter Flex who fell in Russia. They are linked with him in a spirit which is the best pledge of the country's greatness. Here a new Germany begins with deaths, the true beginning for a great cause.

STRANGE rumours are spreading quickly along the front. They are being discussed on every hand and whenever one meets an old acquaintance. They are concerned with the great Rheims offensive, of which much was expected ; and now as so often before in this war when hopes were high, a discreet silence had supervened. It has happened before —more especially, and just in the same way, with the attack on Verdun, of which less and less was said until it died down into a siege and was swallowed up in the thunder of the Somme battle. On that occasion it was all just as it is now. The Army Reports were couched in the same cautious terms ; and yet the circumstances wore quite another aspect. An attempt had been made to come to grips with the enemy and for this, after the German manner, his strongest position had been chosen ; and even supposing the onslaught had not come off, well—it would be followed next by operations of quite another kind which would have shown what we were capable of. It is not so to-day. The circumstances are the same, but they wear quite another aspect.

To-day as I stood in front of my hut and B. ended a long talk with these words—' The show is up. You can be sure of that. Now it is the Americans' turn and they will go for it as we did in 1914 ' —I had a peculiar feeling. I can say without hesitation that for the first time in the war the thought came to me without disguise, ' Suppose then we lose the war——'

It was a quite unprecedented thought, the open expression of which before the conclusion of peace entailed the penalty of death.   But it woke in me all the same and I had surprisingly little to oppose to it ; and I believe it is the same with many others in these days. When you have been for a long while incorporated with an army in the field and linked up by the forces of attraction governing each atom in the whole, you cannot escape the consciousness of all that stirs it. You know that there are secret indications over and above those that pass from mouth to ear or are read in print.

In every battle one learns to recognize these influences that in a fraction of a second sweep men to the crest of frenzy or sink them just as unthinkingly to a perhaps ungrounded despair.   In battle all this happens with rapid alternations under the stress of an excitement that only one who has been actively engaged in it can realize.   The impulse that welds together scattered parties of men who have lost touch with their units is purely a matter of feeling ; and it all passes so much as a matter of course that it never comes to mind again afterwards.   And yet on such occasions a mysterious world is unveiled which is either not realized or else forgotten, just because the pressure of practical activity is so abnormal.

And yet we must beware of regarding battle as a purely practical event, for it engrosses at the same time the utmost imaginable powers of the soul.   Little is said of this in war literature, for the very reason that it is the work of soldiers, men of action whose powers lie elsewhere than in the pen.   But if a being whom no shot could touch and whose feelings were not involved one way or the other were a spectator of these frenzied moments, he would see a strange sight.   He would observe that events did not follow the course laid down for them by the rules and treatises elaborated for the conduct of war ; he would observe that, with the instant menace of death and the entire disregard of life, something quite different entered into the men engaged and filled them with a rage of intoxication.   He would see forces at work that collected at random one man here and one man there from the line of battle to form detachments fighting on their own—forces that linked up friend and foe and came in both to simultaneous recognition.   He would see a body of men come together in this fashion, without a word among themselves or a command from elsewhere, and rush to an attack that would be condemned as madness in manœuvres and yet inspired every participant in it with the certainty of success.   Then again he would observe the frenzy of panic appearing without any apparent excuse and filling whole trenches with hysterical mobs and confused cries that nothing can withstand.   The morally decisive moment of an attack, too, would present a fascinating spectacle—when both sides, whatever their actual relative strength, see the result in its true colours.   Nothing that one can relate of it afterwards is more than a shell picked up on the shore of memory.   It gives only the outer form of the animal that once lived in it.

It is an important task of modern psychology to

study these spheres of activity that invisibly and yet powerfully permeate the mass and magnetize it into changing formations like a heap of iron filings. There are laws here whose workings must be explored. It is not, in any case, a matter of disintegration, but rather of a constructive activity, of fixing a very simple resource that must be put at the disposal of the leader as part of his equipment. For we must learn to practise a kind of demagogy from above, so as to work upon mass-feelings at those very moments when the turmoil of unexpected and critical events puts the most rational appeals out of court and leaves nothing but feeling to work upon. The genius for such moments needs no learning in any case, but talent might at least be trained in dealing with them. This means in the first place that the existence of this immensely important problem must be admitted, and that the prospective leader must be made to look on the men as more than obedient machines. Among all the factors that leadership has to reckon with, the men are the most variable—a fact of which little is heard or seen on the parade ground.

And we need this feeling now, especially when dark rumours go from mouth to mouth and the thunder of new battles draws nearer. It is more necessary to us than any local success in the field.

' Holding out ' has become a catchword, but it is perhaps more in place now than during previous years, when it had too little action about it ; and it must be brought home to the men in its simplest meaning with no historical or economic additions which would be out of place. It is for us junior officers who are most closely in touch with the men to take it up as the

appointed advocates of our country's cause and to be
the medium between the lower instinct and the ideal.
This is more difficult than ever, for whatever is in the
least applicable has long since been ridden to death.
As for myself—for every one must begin with himself—
I shall use our immediate situation as an introduction,
and address the eighty men to whom the company has
been melted down in something like these words :

' I should like to say a few words before we go into
the line.   A few days ago I spoke of the progress of the
Rheims offensive.   I pointed out the coloured lines on
the map that showed how deeply this attack had
penetrated.   I ventured to predict that this old and
famous French city would soon be in our grip.

' You may have wondered perhaps why I have not
been able to give you news of this, and no doubt you
have been discussing it among yourselves meanwhile.
Well—my opinion is that the soldier should not only
be told of the army's successes, but of its failures too—
and there must be failures in an enterprise so vast as
this war.   For he would be a poor fellow who could
not be trusted to know that the cause for which he
fights is in peril ; and it would be a poor cause that
could only find champions while it was under a lucky
star.   It was never the German way to make truth
dependent on the turns of chance and to slip away
quietly as soon as luck gave out.   Only when men
are needed is it known whether a people has them
or not.

' You know well enough that newspapers lie.   They
are written for those at home who have not strength to
look realities in the face.   But you who face the enemy,

and are called upon to make history, can claim that nothing should be kept from you. Complete reliance must be placed upon you, for if there were any doubts here the war would be utterly senseless. Hence I feel, as your leader, that I should be sowing mistrust between us if, as soon as the situation appeared to turn to our disadvantage, I filed the map away among the company papers and behaved as though I had never said a word about Rheims.

'I must tell you, however, that I know as little about these great events as any one else in this company. Little can be made out from the Army Reports. They are read by the whole world and it would be ridiculous to publish the news of a set-back in them. The enemy could say that the importance of their successes was proved by our own admission. But in us, who have no aim but to serve our cause with all our strength, the continual silence arouses the apprehension that our high hopes have not been fulfilled. And that is all that I can say about it.

'Supposing our apprehension to be correct, let us look at it more closely ; for we are used to looking things in the face, however threatening they may be. What would a severe defeat on any part of the front mean to us eighty men who stand here ? And now let us for a moment speak frankly. I know that the morale is not the same as it was in 1914. That is an impossibility after all we have been through. Experience has sobered us, and we are not the same men who in those days marched laughing and singing to the railway station. But that is not what I mean. I am going to say something now straight to the point.

' When we were last in rest we went to see the shell-shot tank near here, as I wanted to say a few words about it.   On this tank, besides the mocking daubs of the English, there was scribbled a number of names and sayings such as you see on the walls of a view-tower.   Of course you read them—as many others will too. These sayings were all in the same spirit.   A year ago they were unknown, and now they crop up in such spots like toad-stools on a tree whose sap begins to fail ; I can only recall one of them :

> We fight no more for Germany's honour,
> But for the millionaires who sit upon her.

' I often go along the trench at night and in this way hear a lot that I say nothing about.   For, just because I am in command of you, I want to hear not only what you say to my face at moments when discipline requires a soldierly bearing, but as well what the real feeling is among yourselves.   And I may tell you that the other day I heard this very saying I quoted just now from the lips of a man of whom I never should have suspected such a thing.

' At that I said to myself that this spirit of doubting must have become very strong, and I feel that I can have nothing further to oppose to it if any one of you in his heart contests what I am saying now.   For one must have belief in one's people and country.   In the old days when we first took the field this belief was strong and unshakable, and we owe to it the great achievements to which we shall always be able to look back with pride.   And I can only beg you to think back to that time and to the vow that most of your

M

comrades have since sealed with their blood. Do not
destroy in yourselves what is the greatest thing you
possess. Everything that demands sacrifice demands
the whole man. And why should one ask anything in
return ? Do we ask a return for loving a mother or a
child with all our hearts ?

'I could give reasons against this spirit of doubt if
there was anything to be hoped from them. But that
would only mean that I should arouse opposing reasons
and bring argument and division into a cause which
unites us all, and thus drag it down to a lower plane.
I will say one thing only : See it in big—not in little.
Look at your country as a whole, not as a sum of
properties of which perhaps you do not own even the
least ; and the people as a great idea, not as a number of
persons, every one of whom has his failings. I know
as well as you that there are those who serve in the war
and others who have a fine time of it while we are in the
trenches. But do we fight for them ? I know, too,
that when we go on leave, we find the talk all of food.
It is considered a worthy aim to get through these hard
times as cunningly as possible, with a belly well lined
and a mind at ease.

'But is this really the highest aim ? I would rather
say that one man who starves for his country's sake—
and we know such cases—outweighs a thousand others
and all the millionaires, for whom, according to that
rhyme, we are fighting, put together. For them we
have never fought a single day.

'But if you ask me why such folk should have the
best of it in these times I could only ask in return :
Do you mean, then, that one should have a good time

in a war ? Such a question is beneath those who fight for an idea. Could any of you for mere money find the moral strength required by modern battle ? Not an officer nor a man could be had on those terms, and if there are men to go again and again under fire and to face horrors that surpass all imagination, that alone shows that it turns on something else than material values.

' When, however, we turn an envious eye on those who make use of times like these to rake in money or to save their lives, we desert the heights to which a great destiny has lifted us and sink to a depth where eating and drinking are all in all. We show that if we were in their place we should do as they do, that we only lack the opportunity or the cunning, that we only carry out by compulsion what ought to be for every man the highest honour.

' An officer who led such men as that would have to conceal defeats from them, for he would know that they would think : " Things are going badly. Why fight for a cause that is lost already ? "

' But you whom many battles have taught me to know have the right answer to give, even though you may not be able to put it into words ; for deeds come to you more readily than words and you prefer to pay your debt to your country with your blood. It is : " How can my cause be lost if I am not lost myself ? "

' And this is the right answer to give.'

So much for the men. I cannot promise myself to put into the foreground any of the economic consequences of defeat such as longer hours and less pay. For what does that come to ? ' Anyway we shall still be alive to see it,' would be the reply, and on that level it would be the only right one.   It would amount to setting up as a social benefactor.

What really makes a people one will never be anything of a material nature.   I cannot imagine any lasting cement between men but feeling.   Only in that can each man be of equal worth and independent of all advantages of mind, birth, or possessions.   Hence it is in feeling that the building up of a people must have its foundation, and if this foundation is there, the rest comes of itself.   But a great deal must be altered in us first.   Something like a miracle must be hoped for—a spirit as strong as the divine grace that welded great communities together so irresistibly in the Middle Ages.

It follows of itself that each individual accepts this structure with his reason as well and shares the destiny of his fellows.   But he will have to fight against the feeling of pointlessness that overtakes every one when he sees his cause declining.   Above all, when the mind has become accustomed to the belief that war is a final decision, a judgment of God, a supreme reason beyond all that seems pointless, whereby the reins of destiny are put into the victor's hands, there is a feeling that one is crushed by the recoil of one's own arguments.

And yet one ought not to allow a disaster to cheat one in the least degree of a point of view that is the sternest and the best.   Should the other side win, it is unquestionably by rights.   Every one who appeals to a decision by arms submits himself to this mighty verdict. Whether a people recognize it or not, it is all one, since in point of fact the conqueror takes right into his own hands.   On this, however, we have the evidence of history ; and it shows that a conquered country makes its own admission of the right of conquest in its profound dejection and its social upheaval.

This feeling of not having stood up to the great ordeal, and of not having been fit to encounter it, is expressed in reforms like those in Prussia in 1806, or in revolutions like those in France in 1871, or in Russia yesterday. It would be a fallacy to assert that a revolution like that in Russia is the immediate cause of the downfall of a country at war. It is merely one of the phenomena of defeat.

One ought not, either, to try to put the blame for defeat on one part of the people. It is always the fault of the people as a whole. For it cannot be too strongly emphasized that in war, and in modern war above all, it is not a part of the people but the whole of it—all its forces and their interrelations—that is thrown into the scales. In all countries where there are sections of society that have a smaller share than others in the common weal there will be weak spots. Hence war is the application of a social test. Behind the smoke-clouds that envelop the two warring armies the people confront one another with all they have and are—knit up in one gigantic being that has its qualities and defects like any individual. When a man ails in any part the whole man is sick. It is the same with a people.

War with its test and strain is the only proof of a country's sound condition. In economic rivalry or the famous battle with spiritual weapons, the apparent strength of a country may conceal the utmost hollow-ness, corruption, or oppression. In war, however, the weak places of this organism will be quickly brought to light.   The test passes from individuals to the whole body of the state.   This is clearly shown by the fact that in war not the least importance is attached to preserving the individually valiant men.

Wars are bound to occur from time to time   In them is manifested that determination of nature to intervene directly in the evolution of the greatest organisms of the earth, though they strive to withdraw themselves from her influence, and to break in forcibly upon their one-sided and purely economic aims. When the distinction used to be made between an outward pretext and an inward reason—by which was always understood certain defined questions of an economic nature—the inward inevitability which is ever the same was overlooked.   For one may leave it to the pacifist to regard the call of the blood as merely the final factor in the competition for markets, raw materials, and oil.   If that were all, and if matters amenable to reason actually played the leading part, then certainly an eternity of peace could be thought probable.

There are only two conceivable ways in which a people can be affected by defeat.   Either its inherent strength is utterly exhausted so that it will never again have any part to play, and its annihilation is only to be taken as the outward sign that nothing further was to be hoped of it—in any direction; or else its inner core remains sound, and then its defeat is the finger of fate convicting it of having entered upon war without being strongly enough organized to meet the demands of its age.   The loss of a war under such circumstances may help it forward just as much as winning it ; and it is to be hoped that in this case we shall find a Stein, a Hardenberg, and a Gneisenau, men of a level-headedness to see what was good before and what must be altered now. For the feeling that a wrong has been suffered must find its expression in this constructive spirit.

Certainly it is easier simply to hide behind the excuse that the enemy was too strong. But that means giving to mere numbers an importance that should always be denied them, more especially by the weaker side. The experiences of life should always be taken as a challenge and never made into excuses. Whether the enemy won by the preponderance of material, whether he stood more solidly behind his cause, whether his workmen showed more intelligence, greater readiness for sacrifices and a closer bond with the state, whether his tactics overcame us, whether he bribed more recklessly, whether there was a deeper patriotism in his leading men, whether he had a better government, whether he had more railways or fewer illiterates—it will always come to a difference which must be overhauled and outbid. In this way alone, and not by talking about it, can the right to conquer be created.

One can imagine a circle of men drawn from all nations, an unmasonic lodge, who would delight in this rise and fall of the waves that exalt first one nation and then another. For the source of those achievements that benefit the world as a whole is to be found in the will that urges all peoples to assert their ascendancy, to strive on in rivalry and antagonism. Each must be for itself if God is to be for all. So soon, however, as everything was stewed up in an international brew, a prospect that fortunately can exist only in the imagination, all movement, all sharpness of form and idea, would vanish for ever together with the oppositions and contradictions on which alone they depend.

Even if we are defeated, the conviction that no world can thrive in which we have not the first place will never be eradicated from the real core of our people. We shall wait and see how the conqueror carries out the responsibilities that have fallen on his shoulders. Our hour will come again, for no one is so strong that he can hold the reins of destiny for ever. Therefore we must set ourselves to a work in which military preparations form only the smallest part. War is no longer a military question. In that direction we shall never be able to mobilize in greater relative strength than we did this time. But there are other directions in which we have not advanced far enough. In every imaginable direction we have severe and grievous experiences to go through, and we shall turn them to good account. We were well prepared, but still not well enough.

Our hour will come ; and then at last we shall see that the loss of this war brought us to our full height. Hard timber is of slow growth.

YESTERDAY evening when we were already standing by to go up the line, the order suddenly came that we were to remain in rest for the time.   The rumour is that an attack is imminent, and the idea probably is not to expose ourselves while carrying out a relief and also to have rested troops in reserve.   So far we have always had to pay dearly for such added days of rest.   I am taking the opportunity to get abreast with my letters.   Here is the draft of one of them :

' Many thanks for your letter.   How go your lungs and your arm ? For once in a way we are in a very quiet part of the line and I have leisure to get over my last wound and to recall the happy days in R.   We are nearly always in the open air and as bronzed as Indians. The sun is good to us and we are having perfect summer weather.   Nevertheless I often envy you having nearly all your time at your own disposal.   It must be a strange feeling to have your active service behind you and to follow your own pursuits at leisure.   Our paths, till now almost one, begin to separate, and now you are free to take your own again.   In any case I do not count the years I have spent out here as lost, by any means, and I am sorry for any one who has not shared in this great school of experience.   It is a great thing to share in one's country's destiny and to be bound up with it in good times and bad.   Thus the fate of all is reflected in one's own experience.   It broadens the mind as nothing else could, and gives, as nothing else could, the feeling of solidarity with one's fellow-men. Indeed I have given up the plan I cherished before the war of going abroad, for I do not want to weaken those bonds that the war has made so close.

' I was interested to hear that you again had military employment—though it cannot have been a very enjoyable task bringing a detachment of recruits such as you describe up to the front. Rifle-fire from the train, wild tumult, mutiny, and threats—it all reminded me of Zola's *Débâcle*, whose scenes I should only have thought possible among the French. I can imagine that you were glad when you handed the men over to their Division, even with a loss of 25 per cent. You might easily have found yourself in a tight corner.

' Your letter made me ask myself what would have to be done if it really came to a conflict on such an occasion. It is not at all a simple matter to enforce discipline upon men to whom you are quite unknown and who presumably have a strong sense of solidarity among themselves. The worst is that there are no precise directions for such a case.

' We have always been so incredibly orderly that we lack experience in this matter. We are without the prophylactics that occasional infection leaves behind it in the blood. I imagine that in France with their wealth of revolutionary experience they are better prepared for such manifestations. The Englishman, too, who has had a long apprenticeship in his colonies and at sea, is not so easily caught napping. We ought to have studied this question, at least in theory. It would have been of service if such possibilities had been no less prominent in our training as officers than, for example, the possibility of a duel.

' On such occasions the officer always has this in his favour, that he represents the right, whereas the feeling of being in the right has first to be worked up by those who oppose him.   I assume, of course, that he has done everything in his power with regard to the outward conditions of the men, their rations and so on.   This sense of right is the true moral factor.   Here, as in every other sphere of life, one must be careful not to let it pass to the other side.   Hence one should not flinch from an open collision, but even invite it if it is inevitable—as it always is when implicit obedience is not met with.   In any case the matter will only be made worse by each outbreak of clamour and confusion.   It has to be disposed of methodically, swiftly, and in cold blood.   For that, one must be acquainted with the forces involved ; and they are almost always the same.

' You will always find three types of the refusal to obey orders.   There are the honest fellows with a grievance, the rotten fellows who invent one, and the mob-feeling that may be led by either.   Nowadays when men are sent to the front instead of serving the heavy sentences on their crime-sheets, one has to reckon with attempts at making discipline difficult or impossible.   In this we reap the direct penalty of our weakness in abandoning, for the sake of numbers, the principle that only the best are good enough to bear arms.   Anyway, we now have difficulties of that sort to reckon with.

' In a case like yours, the right thing, in my opinion,

is to wait till you arrive at one of the larger railway stations where help is available. Meanwhile order the N.C.Os. to arm themselves and, if possible, to call out to two or three of the ring-leaders by name. On arrival at the station, if there is noise and disorder on leaving the train, single out the noisiest and strongest fellow, go straight up to him and make it clear that he alone is meant, and give him a distinct and precise order, perhaps to take off his equipment or to get back into his compartment. If he disobeys, shoot him at once.

' It will never, you may be sure, come to this *ultima ratio*. There will be a dead silence, and a half circle will form round the man addressed, while behind the officer is ranged the whole authority of the state. He will be led away and handed over to the R.T.O. Then the order to march is given with the strictest formalities of the parade ground. Numbering off to form fours is an excellent way of evoking speedily the sense of an organized body. It is a good dodge for reducing the mob to its component parts. The men whose names were taken by the N.C.Os. are then ordered to step out from the ranks and likewise taken into custody at the least excuse. Now is the moment for the officer to improve the occasion by a few telling words if he feels equal to it. If not, better leave it alone. Words are easily overestimated.

' All that is perfectly simple. There is no need at all to be twenty years old, nor of a commanding intellect. Nothing is needed but the conviction of the right to give orders, and this the simplest man can have ; and there is no need whatever to give them in the well-known nasal tone. There is no lack of the power of command among us—only we have not had schooling enough in it. I have always observed that it is most pronounced in officers who have been in colonial service ; and I explain this, not by the fact that they have had natives under them, but that they have been in independent and responsible posts, and forced in early years to develop strength of character. This alone is a reason for colonial expansion.

' I have been reading Macchiavelli again lately. I came upon his saying that states which have had a career of civil war develop the greatest military power. This is intelligible—for in such times each man must see it through for himself. No one is a general except it be by his own personality. In the midst of a mob defying all bonds of order the power of individuality is very quickly felt. But those influences that are becoming more and more prominent since the affair at Wilhelmshaven have more of mutiny than revolution about them. They are quite meaningless—the products simply of hunger and cowardice. Bestial is the only word for them. If they pulled it off they would be in no position to put better men in charge of affairs. And no more need be said. Such fellows have no right to overthrow a state that, taken all in all, whatever we may be inclined to lay to its charge, has so immense and promising a record to point to that its failures are trivial in comparison. If we win the war we have so much before us that this paltry business will peter out of itself, and there will be a place for every one. A pack of spiritual souteneurs and literary gentlemen seems to be associated with these deserters—at a safe distance, and for them the birch will have to be taken down without delay. The German of yesterday, to-day, and to-morrow is this time on the other side, and so no measures can be barbaric and energetic enough. Unfortunately we are not half so barbarian at bottom as the world would make us out. Any one who in this war has any scruples towards ourselves or others deserves to see the war lost, and can make no resistance at all if he is made into a nigger for it. It is no time for tolerance.

‘ We must no longer offer an asylum to all the ideas and ideals that throng to us from all lands. Toleration on all sides, of which we were so proud, must be seen for what it is—a negative quality. He who has no real belief in anything can certainly be tolerant and to spare ; but only intolerance has any force behind it. The conviction that excludes all else, the glow of fanaticism —that is what we lack, the mind made up and set that makes us look back to-day to the Middle Ages with other eyes than those of the Enlightenment, and that of itself inspires us with a still unconfessed longing for the Catholic Church after our atheistic upbringing in evangelical surroundings. The day of enlightenment is over. The war completed its downfall and throws us back of necessity upon feeling. What may we not become, if we are able out of our inner force to set in motion the gigantic manifestations of power that stand at our disposal, and to inspire them with our own vitality ?

‘ An official and officious patriotism, together with the forces that oppose it, must be swallowed up in a frenzy of faith in Folk and Fatherland, blazing out from every rank of society, and every one who feels differently must be branded as a heretic and rooted out. We cannot possibly be national—yes, nationalistic—enough.   A revolution that inscribes this on its banner shall always have us in its ranks—for the state is not our absolute.   Folk and Fatherland were given us at our birth.   We know them for the best we have.   The state is no more to us than the strongest means of substantiating them.   We do not stand or fall with the form of the state, if only for the reason that our folk reach far beyond the geographical boundaries in which the state is comprised.   The union of all Germans in the great hundred-million Empire that is to be is an aim that is worth dying for.   For that we are ready to strike down whatever opposes us.   Far too little stress has been laid upon this, and we know well enough what interests are to blame for it.

‘ But if we survive the war and return to our country once more and find ourselves no nearer the fulfilment of this aim, we shall not let ourselves be so miserably put off as did the young men of 1813.   There shall be no Romantic Revival for us, to switch us off from the burning questions and to veil an impotence for action. We have accustomed ourselves to other ways.   For four long years we have lived as beasts, not as men ; like the hermits who were banished of their own will to howling deserts.   We veterans of material war have become dour.   We bite our teeth into ideas as we do into any bit of trench and are not to be fobbed off by a plausible argument.   These times have bred a dangerous brood.   We consider that the nation’s best are those who face the enemy at the closest quarters, and if decisions of weight are come to in any other sense, no disillusionment could be more frightful. If we lose the war, the guilt for it is not irretrievable ; but if it is lost dishonourably it can only be a crime punishable alike in those who commit and those who permit it. And it is not to let a crime go unexpiated that one gives up four years of one's life.

' But once and for all we shall resolve from the outset to keep our hands clean and to open our ranks only to genuine enthusiasm. When we man the barricades it shall not be in any class war. We shall fight for those things only that bring no material advantage in their train. From those others we are parted by a deep gulf.'

WE carried out the relief yesterday evening after all. The order to do so came as suddenly as the one to stay behind had done. There appears, however, still to be some cause of anxiety, for we had to keep patrols out in front of the wire all night. I scouted round myself with H. for two hours. We heard the English posts coughing but found No-man's-land free of enemy patrols. Now more than ever it does one good to be engrossed in war again. As soon as you go even a little further back, you are got at by a thousand implications, reflections, and doubts. Here everything is reduced to one simple formula.

I have spent so many summer nights in the open during the last years that I can no longer distinguish one from another unless they were marked out by a direct collision with the enemy. They all melt into one memory, and even that will soon lose its salient features. Already when I look through my diaries on leave I find nothing but the technical details of one scrap or another.

Brutal encounters rise again before one's eyes. Swaying figures start out of the darkness in the glare of bursting bombs. Seconds only have to suffice for finishing off one's opponents before the gigantic forces between which one has ventured, as though between two mill stones, have time to get to work.

It has always annoyed me to find all this set down

so drily. I have felt the same with all the accounts I have read in recent years. We have been inundated with such literature, and it must be allowed that it proceeds from a very proper feeling that the war has to be brought home to us in this aspect as well ; but in spite of an inner reluctance I have always returned again and again to the quest for some one who writes of it ' as it is.' Meanwhile I have read in the Lille war journal, and in many other publications, descriptions that, in spite of their accuracy, left a feeling of dissatisfaction behind them.

I used to have just the same experience before the war. In those days I bought accounts of African travel, for those regions made a powerful and mysterious impression on me even as a child. But it was only when I came upon some quite brief travels by a Swede, Jürgen Jürgensen, that I knew what it was to seize the spirit of a foreign land. There were the same primeval forests, wild beasts, and natives ; the same fatigues, dangers, and fevers ; and yet I got my first clear realization of what Stanley and many others had left me groping after. Here at last was some one who understood how to give the soul and not just the husk, so that even one who had never seen these places was forced to say : ' That 's how it must be.' There was something here that cannot be caught, thread by thread and detail by detail—that indefinable something that opens wide prospects in the bare print, and breaks now and then into iridescent lights beyond the gamut of words. There were the facts, too, all in their place, like the little stones of which the mosaic was made. There were no gaps between ; but it was the inner connection that gave the glamour to the whole.

Any one who succeeded in giving a picture of what goes on here would have to do it in this manner, the manner of the artist who recognizes that the reality of feeling is far above the reality of fact. For what actually happens day by day is very monotonous and unvaried, a dull grey sometimes lit up by a gleam of red. Life at any street corner has more variety, and more colour and light in any drawing-room. But in war the feelings are at their highest pitch. Compared with the expenditure of sheer force the amount that actually gets done is very small. It seems that the stuff is of too hard and heroic a grain for the formative action of feeling to get a grip on it.

Certainly the psychological method belongs to psychology or to military science. Perhaps it would mean emasculating a heroic being into a Raskolnikov if one were to analyse the feelings and thoughts of a man going into battle instead of conceiving him as an indivisible unity. It does not suit us Germans ; and we have not, either, the plastic way of describing war experiences, such as a Marbot or a Ségur dispose of. It differs from our way as much as the Arc de Triomphe does from the Völkerschlacht-denkmal. This renunciation of the refinements of form in favour of momentum, of which the last expression is to be seen in the new style of battle that Ludendorff put into effect a few months ago, appears to the Gallic eye as an alien, barbarian, and soulless force. But we who are bound up with it in feeling and experience know what lies behind it.

To set about the picture of the war in this German style would be the best thank-offering of the spirit to fact. What could be done to leave the nation with a proud memory of this time, we have done. It is now for the nation as a whole to see that it is the worthy trustee of this memory. Here the artist, too, will find his account—unless, perhaps, there were no figures in the battle of the Somme to compare with those in the 'Nibelungen Lied.' But was there not as frightful and dramatic a simplicity in this ring of fire and steel where the battle was fought out without a prospect of escape, as in Attila's hall? We can but believe that an understanding of this will be revealed. Or is it that only those times when words themselves are still hard and unworn as blocks of stone are equal to such tasks? Perhaps art has become so anaemic that it confronts us without understanding and even with repugnance. It was already well on the way to it.

Art must become German again, just as we soldiers have only been taught by the war what Germany is. But even though nothing is written about us, the intensity that is bound to pervade every sphere of life will be felt in art too. Problems are bound to change their face, if only because that part of the nation that returns from the war—and this undoubtedly is its best part—will find no more meaning in the state of affairs of yesterday. The horror of those days will be forgotten, but the greatness of their sacrifice will never pass away. In the moral world no force is ever lost. Here, too, there are influences linked up and handed on. They may be hidden but they are powerful none the less.

We have, by chance, a good example of this. In the previous war to this, a young stretcher-bearer was standing in a French village when suddenly the earth shook and a cavalry regiment in closed order turned the corner and went by him in a flash of colour. He said later that this magnificent manifestation of life, a picked body of young and fearless troops representing the will and the justification of a nation's aspiration to power, with death awaiting them, perhaps, in that very charge, made an unforgettable impression on him.

' As they careered past me,' to give his own words, ' into battle and perhaps to death—so wonderful in their vitality and martial courage, so complete in their expression of a race that must either rise to power or perish, I felt that the strongest and the highest expression of life is not the poor struggle for existence but the urge of battle, the urge to power—and overweening power.'   There is no need to say whose words these are.   May our deeds, too, open the way to a new and great and stern conception of the world.

SCHÜDDEKOPF has come back from leave and was greeted by his comrades as a young bridegroom with the usual jokes. I am very glad to have him back as H. has been sorely trying my patience lately. He is really of no use for anything but throwing bombs at the heads of the English, and I am curious to see what he will turn to when the war is over. His military career in any case will speedily terminate, for he is at once the best of fighters and the worst of soldiers. I imagine he will look out for a fresh theatre of war, and hope for the sake of society that he finds it in some of the wilds of Africa.

It is a pity, for the war has shown that we need such desperate fellows, but they are quicker to break their own necks in quiet times than when there is fighting on. They are under the necessity, in fact, every now and then, of letting blood, their own or some one else's, or indeed of going to any lengths ; and of this there can be no question in an orderly society. When they lack education they have no possible outlet for their full-bloodedness in more exalted pursuits. All the same they are fine fellows, true types of primitive life, when you come to know them. There ought to be some means of helping them decently over the intervals of peace and finding them some vent, so that they would be at hand when wanted.

The French have their Foreign Legion as a standing body of adventurers. Algeria, Morocco, and Indo-

China were conquered almost wholly with German blood, and any one who has acquainted himself with the history of these regiments of mercenaries may see from their achievements that the blood which has flowed in this service cannot have been bad blood, even though foolhardy. It would be worth our while to have such a body in our own service. Have we no colonies where such fellows could get themselves knocked on the head, since such is their dearest wish ? These two regiments, which are composed almost entirely of Germans, and adventure-loving young fellows mostly, would have given the English many a hard nut to crack in South-West Africa.

But this is not our way. Can one imagine that we would ever find it in our hearts to dispense with documents of identity, permission of guardians, and previous convictions. There must be some spot, anyway, within our own boundaries, where a man is accepted at his own value, and where his superfluous vitality might be turned to account, instead of forcing it into opposition to the state and to society.

Apart from these considerations of mere utility, it would be a good thing if life in times of peace were in general stirred up a little, so as to make a few concessions to the inherent virility of the nation, and not to cut the link with those passionate and elemental forces which inhabit the soul of everybody. This would also be to our profit in war. Certainly the man who is inspired by an idea makes the best fighter, but passion, too, is not to be undervalued, particularly when one considers the almost sporting character that the extensive employment of machine-guns gives to modern war. A race in whose ordinary life the senses play a prominent part will turn a more eager enthusiasm to bold enterprises like a war. It is easy to see, however, from the growing force of the attacks made upon the death penalty and duelling and even upon self-defence, how far we are allowing democracy to carry us. These are clear indications of our scale of values. It is beyond us to see anything in hardy forms of sport— such as boxing or bull-fighting—but brutality, particularly when their ferocity is knit up with strict and traditional forms. The citizenly need of excitement and suspense is, to be sure, met by a game of skittles. All the same, the time when repose was a citizen's first duty and when the citizen, compared with other forces at work in the state, had become a pure mollusc, will soon be over. These days of very private means are past. But the citizen goes to the cinema, and the cinema must be accepted as a given fact of real importance. There is no doubt that the film offers popular entertainment on a large scale and of a character far from innocuous. It is well capable of purveying highly combustible and sensational matter. For this reason it is already the object of suspicion, whereas it ought rather to be turned to a good use. The film demands action, energy, and power ; and it is not by accident that it draws more and more upon the Renaissance, the French Revolution, and the times of the Caesars. It would be an admirable means of enhancing the modern battlefields. To turn away from this theme or to veil it is already a sign of inward weakness. Gigantic films with a wealth of resources spent upon them, and shown nightly to millions during the only hours of the day they can call their own, would have an invaluable influence. Moral and aesthetic compunction has no place here. The film is a problem of power and to be valued as such. The direct interests of the state are involved, and they necessarily go far beyond a negative interference by censorship. The film is superior even to the Press as a Macchiavellian resource owing to its greater obviousness and accessibility. In both cases there must be a light hand on the rein. The surest influences are those that afford pleasure and are otherwise unnoticeable. A style suited to young ladies, patriotism from above, and that tone in which, in the higher schools, the times of the Roman Emperors are bungled up with the German Middle Ages, or that other in which pedagogues write notebooks designed to take the place of stories of Indians and read by no healthy boys—none of this would be appropriate here. It is painful to others beside the man in the street to run against schemes of education in places where he goes to amuse himself. Food and fun, a strong appeal to the sensual man, demagogy from above (Pericles), with the preconceived idea of directing into this appointed channel forces that are there and must be reckoned with, applied mass-psychology, and a kind of catholic holiday festiveness—this is always far better than the intellectual race with enlightenment in which the state must always come off the loser, and particularly when it starts with a handicap.

The one important thing is that there should be a commanding spirit, for then every method is fruitful, while mediocrity, however meritorious, is foredoomed when times are critical.

WE have passed through stirring days. The period in the line went by without incident. We were in the support line for the first day, glad to be left in peace, when the fun began ; it consisted as usual of heavy shelling for several days, during which one got no sleep. The series of events was as follows :

Everybody knows the mood that comes over troops when they are taken out after a long spell in the line and withdrawn to trenches further to the rear. The pressure on the nerves of the direct proximity of the enemy, of the surroundings, and the incessant readiness for an alarm, vanishes and gives place to a need of repose. True, the possibility of being put in again without warning is always present, but it depends on a longer chain of circumstances than it does further forward, and this calms the feelings which are more at the mercy than may be thought of such half-conscious weighings-up of probabilities. Hence, too, sleep is sounder than it is further forward, where it is so light that the least sound breaks it and the sleeper's hand grasps for his weapons with the habit of an iron necessity ; and waking up resembles the waking on Sunday mornings after a week of hard work. You take possession and settle down. There is nothing much to be done, and so you take to one thing after another, to fill in the time that once more you can call your own. The sections sit about on the fire-steps or collect in groups in front of the dugouts and talk or smoke or read letters. The air almost of a festive occasion relaxes the faces to which weather and fatigue and excitement have given a savage look, and now they resemble the faces of peasants standing by their cottage doors after the day's work. The drawn-out notes of an ocarina are heard from behind a traverse. One is carving the stick that has become the inseparable companion of soldiers in the line, another with a whetstone for his primitive implement is turning the copper driving-band of a shell into a letter-opener that will perhaps lie for generations in some corner of a cottage on the Lüneburger Heath. There is nothing to drink—so what else is there to do ? The unassuming habits of primitive man have regained their hold—lying in the sun and enjoying the mere flight of time, thinking of nothing and pursuing at most some simple art or craft. Life must have been much the same in some lake dwelling after returning from hunting or fighting.

This is the atmosphere that prevails to-day too. I sit in my shirt-sleeves on some sally steps at the corner of Puisieux Alley, lost in a novel, *Little Briar Rose, or A Pursuit round the Circumference of the Globe.* Schüddekopf is squatting below me in front of the dugout and using his factotum of a knife to scrape off the black grease that always collects round the cuffs of my tunic in the course of a long spell in the front line. Above us stands the Verey-light post in a polygonal niche cut in the wall of the trench and approached by a small ladder. He is a bony North-German type, and for two hours has only moved in order to knock out his pipe and light it again. Now and again a grey figure passes this way or that with the long easy step that is customary in the trenches. The air is oppressive and the silence is broken only by a gentle crash when an occasional shell or two land somewhere near. A scent of sun-scorched grass rises over the wide plain, but down here we see only the baked yellow walls where the grains of sand gleam like crystals and trickle sometimes in little rivulets to the floor of the trench, reminding one of an hour-glass. Time seems to stand still. There is a long while yet till the cooker comes—always a joy, partly because we never have enough to eat, and partly because we must have something on which to pin our expectation.

Suddenly the silent one opens his mouth :

' Green light over the Copse.'

Green is the signal during these days for annihilation fire, and beyond that a green Verey light is no alarming symptom. If often happens that the occupants of a trench call on the artillery in order to procure themselves a little respite. It is surprising, all the same, that heavier fire does not come down. Our artillery seems to think, too, that it may be one of those expensive mistakes that occur sometimes. It is not till a second green light goes up, followed by others, that a few field guns open up like little terriers that are always eager for a scrap. Soon they are silent until more Verey lights entice a few more rounds out of them. It is a habit of the gunner to look on these matters with a noticeably cooler eye and to feel their urgency very much less acutely, for the sense of security is squared by the distance from the scene of them.

We are now standing beside the post and looking over to the Copse. Nothing beyond the usual can be made out except a thin dust-cloud above the shattered tree-tops. Apparently isolated heavies are coming down and nothing points to an immediate attack ; but perhaps the hits are so unpleasant, all the same, that some relief is hoped from a shelling of the enemy's lines. Unfortunately there is no signal asking for counter-battery fire—I was hoping one would be introduced—so that this game often takes the form of tit-for-tat, and that is notoriously a long business.

All the same if the situation were a threatening one, the village and we too would be under fire, for the first thing to be done would be to cut off the doomed men from the outer world and all hope of reinforcement. ' Destructive fire ' is the proper expression for what now seems to be going on over there. That is why there is so little to be observed. The heavy shells plough deeply into the earth, and once in a while branches or a tree-trunk are seen to whirl aloft. In earlier days we should certainly have imagined that we saw men flung into the air, but our fancy has since cooled off considerably.

The worst is the sense of responsibility that affects the officer in command and always arouses a mood of uneasiness and doubt. Shall I give the alarm ? Shall I send a detachment forward ? Or simply wait ? A situation may be to all appearance straightforward, but when it actually comes to the point it always gets blurred in an extraordinary way, and there is always the feeling that one may have forgotten some essential point. The most incredible lapses of judgment sometimes occur that can only be explained by this abnormal state of mind. It is as though one had to come to a decision during a bout of seasickness.

The Copse in any case has once more become a focus-point. There is lively telephone communication, you may be sure. After a brief interval an aeroplane appears, circles a few minutes over the scene like an eagle over its threatened eyrie and vanishes in a bee-line again.

Then the first man comes along Puisieux Alley from the Copse—a runner going to battalion headquarters. You can see that he has been under fire. His tunic is torn and the sweat has made white trails down his blackened face. He asks for water and Schüddekopf hands him a water-bottle which he drinks right off. There is little to be got out of him except that the Copse is being plastered with heavies—' dugout smashers ' as he calls them—and that a whole crowd up there are lying on their backs after a dose of gas. He goes and returns after half an hour with an army medical detachment who have breathing apparatus on their backs.

Late in the afternoon they come back again. They carry stretchers on which are men with glazed eyes and scarlet faces. Now and then they put down the stretchers and refresh the sufferers out of little oxygen gas-containers. It is a frightful sight. The big shells emitted carbonic-oxide gas, which found out the lowest spots and had a stupefying effect. Men, too, with bleeding wounds, the bandages showing up like snow on the soiled uniforms, crawl slowly by—only a few, for the casualties are few with these heavy shells. Any

one who is hit by a splinter from them is generally
beyond help. But here and there the force of the
explosion hurls a man against a tree, or a severed branch
knocks him over, or a splinter of flying wood inflicts a
wound. On the spot, where every man takes cover as
best he can, little is seen of all this, but here, with the
casualties going past in a stream, one can see what
effect the shelling has had. Most of the wounded are
so distraught and disordered in mind that they do not
even hear when they are addressed. Others stop and
excitedly reel off a jumbled story and laugh. They
seem like drunken men. I know this state well.
Another as he goes by says that a man has been left
lying further back along the trench. Two men are
despatched and return carrying a man with no wounds
that can be discovered. Perhaps he is gassed, perhaps
a shell-shocked case who has had a stroke ; it may be,
too, that the explosion of a shell has burst some internal
organ. He is laid on a stretcher.

Gradually the traffic ceases. It is already dark and
we are still sitting where the trenches cross. The
afternoon has passed with a surprising rapidity. Our
spirits are low ; for with the darkness the trenches are
haunted by mystery. Dangers seem to multiply and
to creep nearer. How often before an attack or a raid
we have sat together in the same mood. The ration-
party brings an order from battalion headquarters :
' Stand by till 6 a.m. in utmost readiness for an alarm.'
Schüddekopf takes the chit along the trench and brings
it back covered with the signatures of the platoon and
section commanders. Nothing, of course, will happen.
All the same, uneasiness spreads, and in the stillness of

the evening it can almost be felt as a tremor of nerves.
Late at night I make a last tour of the trench.   In front
of one dugout the men are rolling their coats before
fastening them in with their battle-order packs, to which
the mess-tins are then firmly strapped.   In front of
another, a section is standing in the trench.   From the
middle of it can be heard a low voice.   ' So now let me
see every man with his pack in battle-order laid ready
to his hand.   At the alarm every man puts on his
equipment, and his helmet, bombs stuck in the belt ;
and when I whistle—every man into the trench.
Sentries—first number——'

   All seems to be in order.   I stop once more in front
of my dugout and climb out on to the top to have a look
round.   It is so still that the wind can be heard as it
rustles the grasses.   This stillness is almost oppressive.
It would be better if there were at least a shell or two.
I say a few words to the man on guard, to make sure
once more that all is in order, and then go down into
the dugout.

   The air down below is suffocating.   The narrow
space is charged with the heat of the day.   Schüddekopf, too, has prepared for an alarm.   Revolver, map-
case, water-bottle, and a bulging haversack are laid
near my bunk.   I look inside it.   There is half a loaf,
a tin of jam, a tin mug, a pipe, a packet of tobacco, a
toothbrush, and a notebook.   Into the outside pocket
are stuck four egg-bombs and a small, flat metal flask
which I took a long while ago from a dead English
officer.   I sat down as usual on my bed to pull off my
boots—when it suddenly occurred to me that we were
standing by in case of an alarm.   Well, the night will

pass as many another has had to do under similar
circumstances. I turn the carbide lamp low and pull
the blanket over my head to protect myself from mice
and falling bits of earth.

Of course I am so hot with my tunic buttoned up
that I can't sleep. My thoughts begin to wander.
Shall we really be put in to-night ? Oh bosh—why
to-night more than any other night ? There have been
plenty of windy nights like this. We shall be relieved
to-morrow, and then let some other lot be for it. We
have been in the thick of it often enough and need some
rest for once. The procession of casualties that went
by this afternoon is the cause of this feeling of apprehension. It is always the same when we encounter a
lot of fresh casualties with blood-soaked dressings and
those figures on the stretchers with folded hands.
They bring it home to you afterwards. But there is
nothing much to worry about to-night. It is only the
horrible heat of this dugout. It is as close and narrow
as a coffin. And it is a stupid feeling to lie alone like
this under the earth, cut off from every living soul.
How will the men like it if the carbonic-oxide gas
pours in at the entrances ?

The thoughts wander in a maze of such imaginations
among bombs, falls of earth and explosions. But why
can I scarcely breathe all of a sudden ? Oh, of course,
we are attacking a little village in Flanders. You can
see that church tower in flames behind the green of the
trees. And we have run so fast that we can hardly get
our breath again. But we have pushed on much too far
ahead and both our flanks are in the air ; and we are
being fired on with machine-guns, and the bullets are

clearly visible as little white and red dots. We must retire—and as fast too as our legs can carry us. At last we come to a stop in a depression overgrown with scrub. Whizz-bangs fall among us all the time and go up as if they knew beforehand the very spot we were going to jump for.

'Poor Hensch,' I hear beside me in an unknown voice, 'he's been hit now. There's his whole brain.' I look round and see a hateful grey mess spread out on a thistle-like plant as though on a salad. In the middle of it lies the brass fuse of a shell. No, this is no place to stop in. Let's get on. We set off at the run again. As I run, I fancy I have had a blow on the head, and feel as if there was a gigantic hole in my skull. My brain is pouring out and I notice that I have more and more difficulty in putting two and two together. Nevertheless I run on till I get into safety near a field-cooker. A crowd of fugitives have collected there, waiting till the lid is taken off. It falls to me to help the rice on to their plates. Meanwhile, crazed as I am, I hold my head out instead of the plates. Then I let the rice fall on to the plates again and see to my horror that clots of blood are floating in it. With indescrib-able terror I try to mix them in with my hands before the others see them, for I feel that I am utterly at the mercy of their indignation because I am unable to form a single thought, however hard I strive to discover some excuse in my own defence.

Fortunately, before they discover the fraud, I find myself in a gigantic circular hall with a broad copper band all round the walls. I am running round it in a circle. The flooring is only partly laid, so I see through it into a kind of cavity. I observe below a pear-shaped bomb running on little rails and keeping pace with me. Near me on the copper band runs a friend of mine, and we are holding hands ; we are followed by two other runners at unequal intervals. An old man with a white beard and a professorial air stands in the centre and looks anxiously at us.

I am seized with fear and run round the circle faster and faster. Something that I cannot grasp hangs on it all. Suddenly the two behind us turn about and run in the opposite direction. Apparently one is chasing the other, and as the hall is round, my friend and I draw nearer to them very rapidly. Just as we are about to collide with them, the foremost is overtaken and caught. At this moment the bomb below us goes off. There are volumes of smoke—floor boards flying up in the air and wreckage of the roof raining down ; and the last I see is the observant professor's face looking on at this disaster with approving nods of his head. Then the scene changes.

We are on an immense railway track beside which runs a street. The rails glimmer in the red and green lights of signal lamps. Telegraph poles swoop past us. There is the same company as before—two men in pairs and the learned old gentleman. But this time the other two run in front ; I follow them and my friend follows me. The old man is running on my left. The bomb too is there again. It is rolling in a straight course along the road, propelled by a secret mechanism. It is of the same shape as an angler's float and painted, too, with the same red rings. I feel a strange fear lest my friend, who is after me like mad, shall overtake me.

Now he is close on my heels. We are approaching a place where the road crosses beneath the railway. The old man begins to laugh and at the same time to shout in broken sentences : ' The human equation—ha! ha! You see, if one pair is in contact tension arises ; and when two pairs of equal value—a stream of sparks. I have chosen you well. You match to a hair. You understand—the railway lines are an excellent conductor and the bomb is set for contact.'

He shouts a lot more, and everything he shouts has an absolutely satanic logic and makes an impression of perfect reality. I understand and know at once, ' If my friend touches me the disaster is upon us. The two in front have already caught hold of one another, and only this second contact is lacking in order to complete the current and explode the bomb.'

We have now reached the subway. Beneath us the bomb banks with an elegant curve. Behind—my friend shouts ' Stop—you 're leaving me alone. Call yourself my friend, you swine ? '   I stop in exhaustion just over the subway and he rushes madly up.   In vain I roar out to him as he comes, ' For the Lord's sake don't touch me. The most frightful disaster will follow.'   He does not hear and seizes hold of me, while the old man laughs and mocks from the side of the track.   At this moment, up goes the bomb and hurls us aloft amidst rails and splinters and iron girders.

Just as a new picture is about to succeed, I wake up. The carbide lamp is out. It is as hot and dark in the confined space as a baker's oven. I tear the blanket from my face, wrench open my collar and try to get my breath. I often have such dreams in deep dugouts.

They are not pleasant. The bad air and the almost touching walls must favour them. I have transcribed a number of them and they form strange digressions in my diaries.

The blood beats in my temples. I try in vain to get my whereabouts and to come to some conclusion at the same time about a confused uproar to be heard without—abrupt thumps followed by quakings of the earth. There can be no doubt of it—we are being shelled, unless I am still dreaming. Now heavy steps on the stairs and Schüddekopf bursts in : ' Alarm—red lights over Copse 125 ! ' I put on my helmet, Schüddekopf puts on my belt for me, and then I tumble, still half-dazed, up the steps.

It is pitch dark outside, but at least it is cool. There seems to be dew on the grass already. An artillery duel is in full progress. Our front seethes like a boiling cauldron. Above the parapet there is a firework display of Verey lights of every colour. The shattering reports of our guns resound from the village. The metallic roar sounds as though they were just behind the trenches. Interspersed with them is the sudden rushing pitch of shells in our immediate neighbourhood. It is impossible to put two and two together in the hellish din. Once again the sentry shouts down from his post, ' Red lights straight in front.' Immediately after the blood-red signal soars up into my field of vision too. It hangs for a few seconds like a mystic token, like an ill-boding eye in the midst of this witches' Sabbath, and then dissolves in burning tears.

It must have been for situations like these that Napoleon with his genius for brevity coined his phrase of the two o'clock in the morning feeling. It is the eeriest feeling one can imagine—a night like this with its vast array of fiery apparitions over the dark earth, and its tumult of noises that now distractedly lose themselves and rage afar, now leap forward with the closeness of annihilation as though powder magazines went up into the air. Added to all this—the point of danger is utterly undistinguishable. Danger is on every side, blind and furious as an element. Relations with the outer world are cramped up into a tiny space. They reach no further than the hand can stretch. Hence each man feels himself alone and abandoned in the darkness, flung defenceless into an incalculable and pitiless machinery. On top of all this, thought and action are called for. In the space of a few seconds irrevocable decisions must be made. True, everything as a rule is very simple, but what help is that in a state of mind when you can hardly recall your own name? It is exactly the very simplest things that seem to vanish at such moments and to leave no clue behind them. The most intelligent person loses the power to count beyond three. On the other hand, a simpler and more manly kind of understanding, with the support of a firm character, can by a positive miracle step into the gap. It is shown that the being of a soldier rests on doing the right thing at the right moment, and also how seldom this quality is to be found among our contemporaries—victims of an education that develops a one-sided type of mind.

In this case, the matter was simple enough. We were the company in support of Copse 125 and we had seen the signal for an attack by the enemy. Hence we had to go forward. The men were already in the trench, where the excited clamour was occasionally drowned in the explosion of a shell near by. Helmets, rifles, and bombs clatter, section-leaders bawl the names of their men, and further back there are already shouts for stretcher-bearers, while again and again the shortening pitch of a shell whistles over and fountains of earth rain down into the trench. There is a tumult as though a theatre were on fire.

At the intersection of our trench and Puisieux Alley I come upon a section leader, whom I post there to see that the whole company follows on. Then the order to advance is given and makes its way slowly through the commotion. It is a question in what form it will reach the last man if it reaches him at all, but there is no time now to see to that. We find it a relief to be moving off. As long as one can only be going somewhere, though it may be into the jaws of disaster, there is at the least the feeling of doing something to shape one's destiny.

Puisieux Alley is the one trench for a long distance on either side that leads to the front line, and therefore it goes without saying that it is being heavily shelled. As it lies at right angles to the front it is also easier to hit than if it lay crossways to the line of fire. The great thing, then, is to leave it behind as quickly as possible. We go forward in short spurts and make pauses for rest at spots which offer partial cover. For this reason we are strung out from the start in small bunches. Schüddekopf, of course, is behind me, Schmidt also, and H. appears suddenly out of the darkness shouting something unintelligible, though properly speaking he ought to be with his section.

The trench has altered very much in this brief interval. Our feet sink in the clinging earth which has been scattered over the bottom of it and stumble over shoots of earth thrown down from the sides. In some places it is filled in by a succession of heavy direct hits one upon another, and in others where the walls were revetted with faggot wood it is so entirely blocked that we have to go for a short distance over the top. Often it is filled with a thick vapour showing up in white clouds against the darkness, and a strong smell of burning left behind from the explosives makes it difficult to breathe. Like all smells it arouses memories, but by no means of a pleasant nature. Unnumbered moments start to life in our feverishly working brains, memories that do not get near the surface of consciousness, but give to our state of mind an added eerie touch. Now and then a shell flames up close and blinding and the immediate impression of danger chases all others out. Above the horizon, now here, now there, the whirling flashes of shrapnel blaze out, and suddenly with a blood-red glow detach a bevy of swaying smoke balls against the darkness. Shells of light calibre throw up cones of flame above which burning fragments of metal leap in a fountain of sparks. The rapid machine-like beat of their explosions is dominated by the slower and more powerful note of the heavy shells whose cones of smoke spread in huge vaporous silhouettes like the smoke clouds over a volcano.

When we have to leave the trench at spots where it is

impassable we have a full view of the dark and shell-shot plain, and the scene seems almost too portentous to have been produced by human means. By this time we have got on some way, and the Verey lights from the front line almost encircle us in a ring of many coloured fireworks, sweeping on to and round the Copse and lighting up the swathes of smoke that creep along the ground with bright and fairy-like gleams of colour. As far as the eye can see the darkness breaks into patches of flame that in many places cluster like islands of fiery red. Right round the horizon the flashes of the guns leap up and are reflected again from the clouds. They meet round the wide and quivering circle of the sky which the front divides in two, so that friend and foe seem to combine in producing one effect. The impression made by the whole is no longer that rival interests oppose each other. Rather it seems the gigantic work of cosmic forces, melting into one glow what is and what is no more, and leaving to men a miserable insignificance as they chase about through the shadows in obscure and scattered bands.

Since we went for the first time into battle, the struggle has gone out of all scale in its gigantic proportions. When one considers that over this whole field of fire the lines are held by a few hundred men in units melted down by casualties and sickness, and compares the resources that are set in motion against them, one has to marvel at the fighting force inherent in man. Every day is a proof that the will knows no impossibilities. It must be reckoned, too, that the weight rests on each individual man. There can be no thought of being led or overlooked. I have only time now and then when we are passing an utterly flattened stretch of trench to run round and take a look at a broken chain of shadows now lost to sight in the darkness, now flying apart in the light of bursting shells. At a pause in the uproar the rattle of arms, hurried shouts and calls for help can be heard. It is remarkable how stimulating the mere action of running is. Whether it is because the blood circles more quickly to the brain and so allows the perception a freer range, or because there is no time to be afraid—in any case the exertion calls out by degrees a panting truculence that heads straight for the point of danger and sees no cause whatever for giving way before it.

Once I see H. go headlong as a shell bursts and pick himself up cursing and run on ; this happens more than once. We are conscious of danger no longer. We are oblivious of it like a bull who has had the red cloth too long in his eyes. By now one hears those short furious cries that are always heard on such occasions. Later one can no longer remember having uttered them oneself. It is as though one had wind of the enemy by a fine sense that cannot be deceived and that visits one on these occasions when the soul is loosed and otherwise never at all. It is unreasoning and unrelenting. It must find some object to expend itself on, and now senses that the goal is at hand. The utter contempt of death and the boiling rage that put one beside oneself may be accounted for by the frightfulness of the artillery preparation ; and this is the state one is in when it comes to a decision in hand-to-hand encounter—the last and still more frightful circumstance of war.

We have reached a cavity which must formerly have
been a circus where several trenches intersected but
since had been churned by shells into a flat hollow.
It is piled up with shattered wooden revetments,
shivered dugout boarding, and tangles of barbed wire.
We are so close now to the Verey lights that we can get
an idea of our surroundings in this continuous though
fitful illumination.

Close in front is the Copse. Its tree-stumps emerge
like ghosts from a shifting milk-white wall of smoke and
disappear again. A band of shell-fire that whips the
soil high aloft is the last barrier between us and it. As
we leave this hollow we find the first dead body of this
forsaken tract. He is lying on his face with his limbs
cramped together, and we can just see a hideous wound
that seems to have torn away most of the back of his
head. H. bends down to turn him over.

At this moment a loud rushing sound plunges with
incredible swiftness down upon us from above, as
though a flying griffin swooped to rend us. No time
is left to prepare for the burst by throwing ourselves
flat. Already it has hit the slope of the trench with
irresistible fury and hurled us to the ground. Fortunately it explodes straight upwards. The splinters
sweep on over us, and only those that went up vertically
mingled with heavy clods of earth come down again all
round us quite a time afterwards. It is easy to distinguish their sharp metallic ring from the flat thuds
of the lumps of earth. We have come through by a
hair's-breadth. A few feet and we should be lying
blackened and motionless round an extinct crater—
one among those many groups of unknown corpses

which the soldier, as he makes his way through the barrage, often passes by with a fleeting glance.

H. is the first to get up.   He has lost his helmet and his hair is hanging over his bloodless bone-white face. He looks at us with staring eyes and suddenly roars out in a voice that pulses strangely with his blood : ' The hounds.'

This works on us like magic, like a mad contagion at which the last shred of reason is reft from us.   Now at last we begin to feel the enemy as the living agent concealed behind all this stream of violent sensation. We are reinforced by a number of bombers and machine-gunnners, who now press on into the flattened hollow we have just left and form a vociferous crowd. We are all as excited as maniacs ; .even Schüddekopf, this type of North-German calm, utters short unintelligible shouts like the abrupt cries with which coxes encourage their crews at a regatta.

And suddenly in a flash, without a command given or any disposition of forces made, we all begin to storm on to the Copse.   Not a word or a sign even is required. We are no longer individual men ; all are molten in one single being led by instinct, and hence superior at this moment to any conceivable intelligence.   And how could any one in the cool light of reason rush against this wall of fire ?   Such feats belong to impulse alone. No one even hears the swish of flying fragments of metal that whirl past his head at the utmost known velocity.   There is not a thought of ducking or falling flat.   Each man takes his chance.   In one minute we reach the hedge of the Copse.

This moment when the strung-out line of figures

swaying in the smoke comes upon the scene is the decisive moment. Without it, all the fury and thud of machinery that seems to swallow up all else would be a dead and soulless play of forces like the eruption of volcanoes in a desert of craters. Yet a mere handful of men can confirm or annul all the prodigal energies of fire and steel squandered during the night. There is nothing so frightful that man cannot prove himself the master of in the end. And it is just when material resources seem to reach the point of annihilation that his courage and will-power reach the zenith too. The flattened bit of trench that encircles the Copse is passed at a bound and now we are in a thicket of trunks thrown headlong, severed branches, and wire, in which the torn undergrowth is caught up. Our uniforms are rent in shreds from our bodies. But soon the spaces between the trunks are clearer, and the white chalk of the countless shell-holes diffuses a dim light which shows up the trees. The barrage lies behind us. We are surrounded by a calm that is more menacing with every moment. Schüddekopf, H., and the rest have got lost in the thickets. I see near me only a young fellow who came a few days ago from the base as a recruit. He is standing with both arms round a machine-gun. He shouts : ' Where are the English ? ' in the belief apparently that my shoulder-straps are the source of all knowledge.

Just as I am going to reply, a succession of heavy thuds following very rapidly on each other to our right snatch the words from my mouth. Those were bombs, and immediately afterwards a Verey light swishes up and a thin crackle of rifle shots sets in, scattered and irregular, as though a sack of beans were being poured out. Our men must have encountered the enemy. We set off again at a run, stumbling over tree-roots sticking up in the air, and falling headlong into shell-holes, while on every side is the dry crack of bullets hitting the tree-trunks. We must have lost our way, for we find ourselves suddenly on open ground.

But now it seems the others are coming. We see a number of figures with packs who are hurriedly leaving the wood where it runs to a sharp point. They are not far away at all and we shout, but they do not appear to pay the least attention. Only one leaves the rest and comes towards us and then stands still. His shadowy outline shows up dimly against the sky which is tinged with the first grey of dawn.

But what 's this ? I grip the arm of my companion tightly and we sink slowly to the ground. We were within an ace of walking right down the enemy's throat, when at the last moment I recognized the flat helmet that they wear on the other side of the line.

' Tommies.'

' Fire ? '

' Fire away.'

The gun begins to rattle out till a little yellow flame dances before the muzzle, and the sound of it restores our feeling of confidence and boundless fury. The single drum is empty in a few seconds. Have we hit them ? We can only hope so, but know nothing ; for the phantoms have vanished. We strain our ears to catch the cries of the wounded, but our ears sing with the reverberations of the shots as though metal strings vibrated in our brains. The best we can do is to creep back carefully from shell-hole to shell-hole into the Copse again, for dawn is beginning to break.

The Copse is now full of life, for the whole company has forgathered there bit by bit. Platoon and section commanders are trying to collect their men, but cannot make themselves heard. An over-excited clamour and shouting drown their voices. It is like the dead end of an orgy when a bleary stillness succeeds to an already flickering elation. The nerves cannot be calmed all at once.

The barrage has ceased. The loud popping of a few light guns that appear to be placed just behind the trenches makes an almost calming impression after the tremendous symphony of the night. Between the splintered trunks that stand like the pillars of a ruined cathedral we can see the sea of shell-holes, like a tempest turned to glass. It recalls those stories of unholy spots whose hellish racket vanishes in smoke at cock-crow. The wide expanse is pitted by innumerable shells whose imprint has been fixed as though in a brownish sealing-wax. Far and wide, like the wreckage of a ship sunk in a storm, is scattered a wild medley of objects whose random profusion increases the impression of utter abandonment. Tanks riven by direct hits or rearing upwards, jammed in enormous shell-holes, cast-away packs, riddled helmets and dixies, jam tins, tattered overcoats and blankets, corpses of men and horses—the whole scene looks like the contents of a second-hand shop scattered abroad in contempt of their value, or like the rubbish heap of a gruesome factory that subjects everything in the world to its processes and then spews it out again broken and disregarded.

After living for a long while in such surroundings that may perhaps be a unique and never-recurring phenomenon, one is compelled to find humour and horror linked in the grotesque. All three find expression now and then in a personality of callous cynicism, unthinkable in any except those for whom death is decreed. It is, however, deserving of remark by any who would understand his fellow-men.

There is something grotesque, too, in the clamour and crazed vivacity of the men in their torn and mud-smeared uniforms and with faces masked by a crust of blood and smoke-grime. Their spirits, wrought up by the excitements of the past night, are in sharp discord with the frightful dreariness of the surroundings. They remind one of a band of drunken men in the grey light of dawn. It is, however, intelligible. Every one rejoices to find himself alive, and is incapable of changing himself at a blow from a creature led by wild instinct into a calm and rational human being. Veiled by all the resources of up-to-date battle, the emotions of last night are the same as they always were and will always be.

All the same it is high time to introduce order if a disaster is not to follow We must occupy the edge of the wood, find who are missing, establish communications, and report to battalion headquarters. An enemy machine-gun is getting to work already. It shows that they have got the hang of things and we are forced, now that we begin by degrees to know what danger is, once more to take up a position in the trenches. As it happens we have casualties while doing so. A man falls over backwards with that frightful long-drawn groan with which the life-breath leaves the body at one gasp. Another begins to cry out piteously and has to be carried carefully into the trench. He is found to have a severe wound in the upper part of the thigh.

While we are busy binding up the wound, V. and K. come up, accompanied by two bombers, to thank us for our prompt support. We light cigarettes and exchange our news. I hear that yesterday afternoon's artillery preparation by shells of a calibre heavy enough to destroy the deepest dugouts was followed in the middle of the night by a terrible bombardment—upon which they sent up red Verey lights. As it was unthinkable to keep a single man out in the Copse during this avalanche of shells, the whole garrison collected in the deep dugout where there was still a lot of gas, and awaited developments, some on the steps, some in the entrances. Two of the entrances were hit and had to be dug out again. In the others, too, there were casualties from splinters and shrapnel bullets. When the fire lifted over the Copse the men were distributed in shell-holes in the open. By the light of the Verey lights they fired on some shadowy figures gliding across their front, but beyond this no more movement was observed, and V., when he heard our bombs to the rear, thought he was surrounded. The casualties were fewer than might be expected from the mass of stuff that fell over the Copse. On the other hand, of the men who were in the advanced posts not one has so far got back, and it may well be that not one is alive.

Next I make inquiries of the men who threw the

bombs.   They too had only seen shadowy figures, who forthwith vanished.   It is clear that the attacking party can only have been a patrol, which was either sent out to get bearings for a bigger enterprise or else on the chance of a successful raid.   The puzzling part is the lavish expense of munitions compared with the small-ness of the attacking party.

'They can't have blazed away half a war-loan for fun,' I said.

'We don't talk of fun here nowadays,' growled V.

'Yes, but they must have had some purpose in it.'

'Purpose?' V. replied.   'Listen to me.   How would you like every night as pleasant as last night? You've had a jolly old picnic in your section A. Here we haven't had a night's peace for the last four weeks when we've been in the line.   You've noticed, I daresay, that the English artillery has longer wind than ours.   And the English have something else but mangolds in their guts.   Beside that, there's a fresh regiment every fourteen days over there.   As they can get no change out of a big offensive, they are trying to crumble us down like stale cake, and that in the end comes to the same thing.   I don't deny they're practical, and if they can smoke us out it spares men. Last night it was only a small detachment—to see if we had crumbled yet.'

It may be so.   No doubt it is so.   Precisely for the English, who have little experience in the employment of large bodies of troops, this way of carrying on is the best and the surest.   And as after the great offensive, when the earth seemed once more to revolve at our behest, and when we gave the first example of the employment of modern resources in battle, the power of the initiative was wrested again from our grasp, we have to adapt ourselves to these methods whether we like it or not. It is remarkable all the same that the war that began with so intense an energy is once more to see the strategy of victory in the field replaced by the Louvoisian strategy of attrition. The exhausted lion is still found too dangerous to bring into the open by extensive operations.

At about ten a runner appears from battalion headquarters with orders to withdraw to a position in the artillery defence line. The company files out by platoons along Puisieux Alley and leaves the Copse behind.

' See you again,' V. calls out after us, and I call back : ' But not here, I hope.'

In clear daylight we can see for the first time the full extent of the devastation caused by the shellfire. Now it is over, one asks again and again how we ever succeeded in getting through it. We pass the dead body again in the little hollow. It has since been flung from the parapet into the trench, so that man by man we have to step over it.

It is getting warm by now. The larks sing above the parched expanses of grass. No shelling seems to put them out. The intoxication that inspired the men after they broke into the Copse has disappeared, and a mood of utter exhaustion and ill-humour takes its place. Each man shambles along between the walls of the trench, withdrawn into himself, and every time there is a stoppage or one barges into another this illhumour is vented on the man in front. I can't help thinking of the time when one used to give the beautifully made bed a punch or two at early morning to make the landlady believe one had slept in it, and I promise myself to live a snug and orderly life after the war.   My hunger for adventures is for the while amply satiated.   I anchor my momentary views of life to that devout thought that expresses the utter opposite of all romance and resounds incessantly on every side and in every tone like a Thibetan prayer.   Behind me is the recruit who was so handy with his machine-gun when we had our glimpse of the English this morning.   His face is as white as a child's who has not slept.   It is his first ' show ' and I ask him :

' This isn't how you fancied it would be at the depôt ? '

' Oh Lord, sir, I thought it would have been far worse ! '

I have to take note of the young fellow.   He seems promising.   His remark reminded me of the first time as an inlander that I saw the sea.   I thought the waves would have been at least a hundred feet high.   A youthful fancy makes great claims on the actual.   But this was how we were too when we first came out. Nothing could be wild enough for us.   And when we went on our first leave this over-weening courage, that flinched from nothing, would come on us again.   However highly you may prize the steady and disciplined fighter, he is not to be compared with the man in the first ardour of enthusiasm that gives a unique glamour to the exploits of youth.   In war, as in all else, great achievement calls for superfluity of strength, a wild and demoniac urge to action that characterizes vigorous races.   Obedience is the unconditional duty of armed forces as a whole. It embodies conscious resolution. Enthusiasm is unconscious, beyond compulsion, and in it lies all that can be called the future. The greatest tasks that life imposes are not carried out by hard work alone. There must be some pleasure there that makes the work enjoyment. It is not for youth to decide for peace or war ; but a country is in a poor way when its youth is not eager for action, and eager to come forward for every war that may arise. Victory calls not for strength alone, but for a frothing overflow that is always ready to ask : ' What does the world cost ? ' and makes no scruple about giving the first blow. This is where the justification for dominion lies. It cannot be demonstrated. It must be known and felt as undemonstrable.

The artillery defence line cuts Puisieux Alley a few hundred metres behind the main support line. Just where they cross several tracks lead to the deep dugouts, in which are battalion headquarters. Round the entrances there is a continual coming and going of orderlies and runners, like bees round a bee-hive. The dugouts of the defence line are miserable affairs ; a few steps only lead down to them and the overhead cover is scarcely a metre thick. The air down below is bad and stagnant. There are hundreds of these shelters up and down the lines, disused and abandoned until some alteration in the disposition of the troops suddenly brings them into requisition. Before we can settle ourselves in, the company has to be told off again, the cooker sent for, the gear we left behind in the support line brought along, reports written—in short, a whole array of details that seem of no importance and yet take half the day, has to be got through. At one o'clock dinner comes along, and half an hour later I am so far through with it all that I might have turned in for a sleep if the alarming noise of a fresh bombardment had not sent me out into the trenches again.

From this spot the Copse is hidden behind a rise in the ground. But I can see the village in its whole extent and its gardens come right up to our trenches. Shells are falling over it like a tempest. The small detachments that occupy the meagre cover of the still undestroyed cellars must be having a thin time of it. Now and then the furious storm of shells is dominated by an explosion of outstanding force, and then the splinters reach as far as where we stand and bury themselves with a smack in the earth. The shells appear to come from a good way back. They rush in swarms through the air with a soft insistent whisper that flows on incessantly as though a reservoir were being filled. The shells from the German batteries, on the other hand, close up to and behind the village, hurl themselves into space with a shrill deadly screech. The sky seems to be crossed and recrossed by a network of power and velocity that dazes and stuns the senses. In No-man's-land, too, explosions throw up a brown haze of earth. Some of the shells burst upwards as straight as poplars, others expand in mighty and irregular shapes like old oaks, others again shoot out low over the ground like dense undergrowth scoured earthwards by a storm. The scene is one that nature can scarcely show in its mightiest phenomena of storm, hurricane, or conflagration—one can watch it without knowing how time passes. Two men leave the village, runners perhaps, and go forward over the open ground. They seem to the mere onlooker to be dwarfs in a fairy tale. Now and then they throw themselves down and a second later the earth flies up close beside them like a blazing torch. They make their way like ants over this scene of devastation. At last they drop into a trench.

The weight of fire still increases. The keen whistle of the shells unites in one sound without leaving a gap, closing up in continuous web of sound whose edges are torn to shreds by incessant crashes. The two artilleries are locked in breathless conflict, striving in a crescendo of fury to swallow one another like two gaping hells. The monotonous rolling and pounding seems to have become inherent in the landscape, and the clouds of fine dust, which vanish in the rays of the sun, give it a sullen and menacing air. Storm-beaten islands rise from the thundering breakers of noise— Puisieux-au-Mont, and further to the right, Bucquoy, and, over the hill but unmistakable, Copse 125. Volumes of white smoke are streaming out of the village, boiling up in convulsive flares from time to time. The traffic of walking wounded and stretcher-bearers between the Copse and the village has ceased. There is not a living being to be seen. The raging vortex of annihilation has reached a pitch that puts any movement of troops out of the question. Consciousness, busied hitherto in recording and arranging impressions, begins to give up the task and to merge with the death that encloses it within an orb that has no top and no bottom. The point has come to sit in a corner and stare at the ground as though one had lost the last link with circumstance.

At this moment a runner arrives from battalion headquarters and shouts in my ear orders for an alarm. I go back with him to the big dugout in order to hear in person what is up. It is only a few steps away. At many spots in the trench lie the dead, and the severely wounded men among them show by their expressionless faces that they have given up all hope of coming through. Where Puisieux Alley reaches the highest point of the rising ground, there is a view of the front line. A dense wall of smoke and dust rests upon it, and over this spurts up a firework of coloured magnesium lights. The dugout, one of the few remaining spots where consciousness still survives, is overcrowded with men. Wounded moan piteously on the steps where they have been set down for the time by the stretcher-bearers. Among them, crouching together, is the crowded mob of detached troops who always collect like animals in a flood on the islands of comparative safety. They are made up of stretcher-bearers, signallers, intelligence personnel—of all, in short, who live on their own in the waste and are not kept to their posts by solidarity with a compact body. Isolation deprives them of the power to withstand the flood, and so they are swept along like driftwood and collect wherever there is a refuge. The atmosphere is one of flatness and discouragement. Anxious observations are made in low tones, drowned by the loud outcries of the wounded, whenever a particularly close and violent crump shakes this cavernous refuge and makes it tremble like a ship in distress.

Here beneath the surface of the earth, by the light of candles that are constantly blown out in the rush of air following upon the explosions, is found the human counterpart to the hideous orgy of material raging without. The throng of grey figures, through which runners squeeze their way in a constant coming and going, recalls pictures by Brüghel. There is a mood of depression as though a death sentence were being pronounced. Men of all temperaments alike have lost their senses—the phlegmatic man hunched up and staring before his nose, the sanguine ready at any moment to give way to panic or to start it, the choleric man cursing loudly at every fresh hit and the melancholy man bemoaning his fate. The uppermost dug-out frames are already smashed in like match-boxes. At every fresh crash sand and crumbled soil shower through the timber and drive those who are standing on the top steps down upon the crowd below, causing a stampede in which the wounded are trodden on and the tumult pushed to its last pitch. It is the pulsing of horror pumped in from without and meeting no resistance.

When a hundred senseless men are pressed together as in this dugout shaft, there is no use wasting words on them, and so I am compelled to make my way down like the runners, stumbling, that is, over heads and bodies without heeding curses and outcries. In the dugout itself the throng is not so wild, presumably owing to the presence of the C.O., who may at any moment issue fighting orders. Nevertheless it is still no easy matter to elbow one's way on. Runners and patrol commanders are trying to make their reports ; others are waiting to be dismissed ; the Adjutant, the commander of the machine-gun company, the artillery liaison and intelligence officers try to get on with their jobs in various corners. Dust, steam, and clouds of tobacco smoke condense the light from the candles to small and flickering yellow orbs.

The C.O., who has had no rest for twenty-four hours and may not have for as long again, is seated at a small table. One can see in his face what an ordeal he has undergone in this hellish hole. Apart from the noise of the bombardment, dull and confused and yet menacing as the breakers of an invisible sea, apart from the continual crashes that shiver the timbers of the shaft and from the outcries of the men wedged in the narrow stairway, he is kept in a constant agitation by the contradictory reports from the runners and wounded men passing to the rear who, still hypnotized by their own impressions of the fighting, strive each to portray a different picture of the situation in hectic colours and distorted outlines. All communications have long since been destroyed—telephone wires cut to bits, signalling apparatus smashed and smothered, pigeons used up ; and so, shut off within rings of fire, all feelings but those of insecurity and uncertainty are stunned. Shut off like this, and confined to an obscure corner which no perception of events enters except through the reports of over-excited brains, a commanding officer tackles his problem under the most impossible conditions and with nothing to go on but probabilities and vague intimations of the actual facts. So far, no method has been found of equating either the spatial or mental conception of the fighting unit with the effects of long-range weapons, and thus it is precisely the intermediate command that finds itself reduced to impotence in the most critical moments of the battle.

After reporting, I am informed of the situation as at present known. It is not very cheerful. The enemy has broken through on the front of the regiment on our left. The report of this was sent first to the battalion headquarters of the other regiment and thence here ; so this occurrence must be at least two hours old. Besides this, the line has been bent back at that point, and the enemy is now held just in front of the main support line ; communication trenches blocked and bombing engagements in progress. No reserves are available but my company, whose strength for a long while has been that of a platoon at war strength.

I came, too, upon Dohmeyer and Kius who have reported for orders. Dohmeyer was sent out to get precise information as to the position on our left, but he was caught in some frightful shell-fire in which he lost the men who accompanied him and was wounded himself in the hand. Kius told me of a determined bomb attack by the English. I hear from him that our little shelter where we passed so many hours during the past weeks is in their hands.

' Things are bad,' he whispered. ' Here, have a drop to buck you up. I have still kept hold of this bottle. I don't know whether I 'm on my head or my heels. When they came the first thing I did was to snatch a bomb out of a bundle in which all the strings were tangled. When I saw that they were smoking, I had only time to jump behind a traverse before they went off. Then I pulled the string of a bomb and began to count twenty—twenty-one, twenty-two, while I swung it as if I was on bombing practice, and I should have gone on counting till it went off, if some one

behind me hadn't shouted, " Chuck it—chuck it ! "
And in the commotion somebody pulled the long fuse-
cord of the bursting charge which was still in position
in the trench, and two of our fellows went up in the air
—I tell you, it was a madhouse—you 've no conception ! They 've got us properly in the soup again.'

' Yes, yes, they 've got us again where they mean to
have us,' asserted mournfully a voice behind us.

' Well, if we only get out of this——' said a third,
betraying a doubt whether we ever should. These three
utterances are pretty much what is said a hundred
times in a regiment on such occasions.

Now a new arrival pushes his way into the narrow
space through the human block. He is wounded and
not yet bound up. The wound is concealed by his hair,
and the blood from it has poured down one side of his
face and down his tunic in streams, and trickles as far
as his boots. Apparently it is still flowing, for he holds
his head over one shoulder to keep his eyes clear. He
has a helmet in his hand ripped by a long groove.
There is something fine about him, in spite of the
frightful state he is in. He shows by his bearing and
the gleam in his eyes that he is not one to be sobered
down by the sight of blood but rather to be fired by a
first sacrifice to the war god. The dim light from the
candles gives his blood the dark colour of almost black
flowers and makes reflections on his hair. Among the
crowded cave-dwellers he appears like an ambassador
from a freer and braver race who would rather die out
there in the open if he has got to die after all. His
report too, made briefly in soldierly fashion, sounds like
a last salute from warriors who have fallen like men in

a stubborn fight with no other vision but their duty before their eyes.

' Sir, I report that Copse 125 has been taken. Lieutenant V. and Lieutenant K. have died, shot through the head. What remains of the company have entrenched on the edge of the wood and are holding the enemy in the new position. We need bombs and machine-gun ammunition.'

There is not a sound, and even the wounded listen in silence For us all the Copse has been the epitome of our whole front, a symbol like a tattered flag in earlier days. And just as in those days a flag was more than a stick with a bit of frayed silk nailed to it, so for us this shell-shot and battered bit of ground has been more than a spot without a name to which was given a number to distinguish it from any other. Most of us are plain men, who if we were asked about the war situation or its high aims and implications could only give confused answers. And if any one were to tell them that the losing or keeping of such a worthless bit of ground was of no significance they would have little to say in reply either. They would feel, all the same, that this spot meant more than a mixture of chalk and sand, dotted by shattered tree-stumps, whose position and circumference can be found and measured on the map, just as the cross that many of them wear on their breasts means more to them than a piece of iron with a silver border. It arouses memories in them of fatiguing marches and laborious weeks, of night guards in which this bit of ground rose up like a smelting furnace from the darkness, of days during which it was seen beneath its pall of smoke. Its name would not seem like any other name, but as one that has been branded in the memory and as a conception embracing such a sum of acts and feelings that at the naming of it everything else sinks to nothing as at the sight of a mighty monument. They would feel, too, that the Copse can be no spot like any other, because every step trodden there had to be purchased with blood, and because here the destiny of nations was lived and suffered in the destiny of each single man.

But what has been sealed with blood can be felt only in the blood again. Great conceptions— history, honour, loyalty, manhood, country—that seem in the changing light of reason cold and soulless, have their origin and their enduring life in the blood alone. Here alone is the basis of a nation's solidarity and the unspeakable consciousness of right with which the soldier takes arms in his country's cause, whatever the reason he may give. The blood has its own behests and fashions for itself its own right that is superior to every other conceivable sort of right, for in it lies hidden the right not only of to-day and to-morrow, but of generations long gone by and of those that are yet unborn. Hence it is that there is a wisdom about all the words and thoughts of a man who offers his life without regret. The living force of the blood must be alive in an army if the men of to-day are to make sacrifices for their country such as are only conceivable in view of a past that has been worthily handed down and of a future that must be won in battle. Only in such an army have signs and symbols a meaning ; and the understanding of them is an inheritance and a birthright, from which the bloodless troop of intellectuals are for ever shut out. What the loss of the Copse meant to us can be comprehended in this spirit, in this sense alone.

It is true enough that the grim monotony of the battles of material force make the feelings blunt and insensitive. For all that, there are moments now and then as significant as a brief lull in a hurricane when the veil of insensibility is rent and gives a glimpse of all that lies beneath the surface. There was a hint of this in what the messenger from the survivors of the Copse said just now. It had a ring of a sentence delivered by a higher power, but a sentence of whose severity there was no cause to be ashamed.

The C.O. begins to dictate brief orders to the Adjutant, who takes them down on chits. Of these I receive one. It is short and simple. I am to carry ammunition to the men at the edge of the Copse, and then to take my company as far as Elbinger Alley in order to close our front to the left. For the time being there can be no question of recapturing the Copse. In this maze of trenches that is crumbling up on every side it is quite enough with the handful of men available to see that our front does not give way altogether.

And so we set off once more along Puisieux Alley. There is a fresh crop of dead there whose faces and uniforms are covered with a grey dust that has settled on them during the bombardment and drunk up their blood. The shelling still continues, but it is no longer massed on single points in support of concerted operations. It is distributed over the whole field of battle like a storm that beats up and sweeps on in big bursts of rain. We soon realize, however, immediately after crossing the support line, that the Copse outlined with its bare poles against the setting sun is no longer ours. Puisieux Alley in almost its whole length leads straight for the Copse, and the clatter of machine-gun bullets striking the top of the trench from left to right and singing past our helmets announces that our advance is observed. We are forced to go from bend to bend in short rushes, man by man, and to get over the long flattened stretches on our hands and knees. The succession of sharp reports, like the clapping together of stout boards, accompanies us without ceasing, and it is more harassing to the nerves than artillery fire, since it is the direct expression of the enemy's murderous intentions. The men who have to drag boxes of ammunition and machine-guns occasion stoppages that increase the tension. The exposure of this approach trench, the only one available, shows in itself how little power of resistance we have left.

At last we reach a point from which we can proceed on our feet. We have to make as little noise as possible, for the enemy may be close at hand. Cautiously, with wide intervals between man and man so that each has a field of fire on all sides, we pass along a low bit of trench where the stubborn fight for the Copse appears to have been fought out to the end.

It is one of those infrequent spots where the decision still lay actually between man and man, where each fighter looked his opponent for a few seconds in the eye while there was nothing between annihilating or being annihilated with the utmost possible immediacy and terror. It was abandoned by the survivors and left to its grim confusion and desolation. In the dusk it has the appearance of an arrested dance of death.

What passed in those seconds is as clear as an open book to the eyes of any experienced fighter.

Every shell-hole is full of German stick-bombs and the black oval grooved bombs of the English. Whole boxes of bombs lie on the sides of the trench. They have been hastily torn open and their contents are scattered on the ground. Everywhere among the shell-holes are to be seen the shallower charred depressions where bombs exploded in the stampede of hand-to-hand fighting. The effect of the bursts, which at this range can fling a man in the air to come down like a sack, can be seen from the dead bodies lying all about beside and over one another just as death cast them down. Their faces and bodies are riddled by splinters and their uniforms burnt and blackened by the flame of the explosive. The faces of those that lie on their backs are distorted, and their eyes wide open as though fixed upon a disaster from which there was no escape. Horror is fixed there like a mask—and one that no fantasy could devise. These are the corpses of those who in the retreat from the Copse had the pursuer so close on their heels that bombs were lobbed over their heads to fall at their feet. In their last moments they saw themselves cut off by a flaming and concentrated annihilation. One of them still clutches a stick-bomb, showing that as they ran they let them fall behind them so as to cover their retreat with a barrier of fire ; but that did not suffice to ward off their fate. Where the last of them is lying a great heap of shining brass cartridge-cases is piled up in front of a huge shell-hole. There the machine-gunner who brought the English to a halt must have lain and fired. He cannot have had time to distinguish friend from foe while he swept the trench clear. He must have simply fired into the thick. He achieved his purpose. They have nearly all fallen on their backs, staring upwards, but with a quite different expression on their faces.

The last of them lies behind a low rampart of sand such as children heap up with their hands on the beach. Arrow-like missiles and long empty cartridge-cases are strewn among the dead bodies. Apparently they defended themselves with rifle-grenades and rifle-fire, but they were no match for the machine-gun's scourge of bullets. At the junction of this shell-hole line with the trench, along the edge of the Copse, lies the leader of this storm-troop, the last, perhaps, to fall. He still grasps his Colt revolver. No wound is to be seen on his body. The faultless uniform and the tightly fitting officer's belt and shoulder-strap stand out in contrast with the confusion and desolation all round. He has not even lost the cap that he wears instead of a helmet. Bending over him in the failing light, I see from his badge that he belongs to the Otago Regiment. His face stares grimly into mine. His teeth are bared between blue lips. A stout fellow. He must have charged this bit of trench like a lion.

But this is no place to stop in. It is as though a raging element had been suddenly arrested, like a volcano that a moment since was in full activity. And then it is hard to believe that these dead, who but now were at the most furious pitch of life, and who now lie as though touched by an enchanter's wand, are for ever beyond all thought and will. They are beings after all and not mere objects, and over and over again one steals a look to make sure that they are really lying quiet and without a movement in their places. One is inclined to attribute secret and malicious intentions to the silent and human-seeming inhabitants of this spot. They are subjected to laws so utterly unknown to us, and one is not certain that these intentions of theirs may not be carried out. Nothing that might occur here could surprise one. It is not the noisiest hours of battle that are the most uncanny.

On the right of this trench branches off the trench along the edge of the Copse. It cuts the ground like a ravine, and follows what the shells have left of a hedge that borders the Copse and that may in former days have enclosed a meadow. We have only to move stealthily on for another fifty metres to come upon the occupants of the trench, who are just in strength enough to hold a block hastily thrown together. They have filled a stretch of the trench with barbed wire, and behind this they have knocked in the walls of the trench and built up a rampart across it with the soil. This strong-post is flanked right and left by a few riflemen posted here and there in shell-holes. A dugout-shaft a few paces behind the block forms an important support to these well-contrived defences in which the best has been made of hard straits. In this shaft those of the men not on guard have dug themselves shelters. A supply of bombs is heaped up in front of it, so that they can be passed along from here to those engaged in fighting. Naturally, this small but resolute force has rallied round the personality of one man—a young sergeant-major who stands at the entrance of the shaft. I have known him some time, for he was wounded at my side in Flanders when we were advancing on the ruins of Langemarck. I am glad to find that he at least is still alive. Here, too, he has shown himself a worthy counterpart of the English officer whose body lies behind us at the junction of the trenches.

We have to greet each other in whispers, but in any case the scene itself suppresses all thought of loud outspoken talk. A few yards in the other direction the trench is barred by another block, and behind it too there are armed men in ambush. The enemy is so close that the least thing may prove fatal. We go back together to the junction of the two trenches where the carrying party are waiting and give them directions where to put down the boxes of ammunition.

I learn that V. and K. had already fallen where Puisieux Alley leaves the Copse, both shot through the head by rifle-shots. I recall the ' see you again ' they shouted after me this morning in the Copse, and I am told in reply to my question that a recovery of the bodies is out of the question. It always affects one with painful astonishment to hear that a man whom one saw a short while ago in full enjoyment of all his energies is now struck out and gone. It seems incredible, and it is impossible not to go on thinking of him as still living. It seems as though something were missing, as though something of one's own personality were lost, and this feeling is best expressed in the words, ' As though it were a bit of myself.'

' Do you think then that you can hold out here ? ' He replied : ' Sir, I have only twelve men, but they are men I can rely on—they are good ones. To-night we can carry on, for the Tommy doesn't know yet how we are situated, but to-morrow early——'

Yes, to-morrow early we may be for it, if we get no support, and it looks as though we were left to our fate in this mouse-trap. A feeling of being marooned rises up and catches the throat. I go on in a whisper in case the English officer lying at our feet might hear.

'What about communications? Are you in touch at all?'

He whispers back: 'There is another section of our company in Puisieux Alley. But there is at least five hundred metres between us and them unoccupied. I sent a man along to our left an hour ago but he has not come back. I'm afraid there is nothing doing there.'

To the left? Why there—there is Elbinger Alley. We may be all right to-night yet. A vague feeling of hope induces me to ask again:

'Not come back? What if he went back as far as the field-cooker?'

'No, no. That is out of the question. It was Lieutenant V.'s runner. One of the best men we have.'

Well—in that case. One of the best men. In Elbinger Alley, just here, opening out like a dark menacing gateway as the fourth arm of these cross-ways? Not come back again? Yes, this certainly seems as though not every one need come back who ventures along it. How do our orders run? To proceed as far as Elbinger Alley and make our position secure to the left. Why not, then, make a block just here and sit behind it?

No, it wouldn't do, even though probably not a word would ever be heard of it. But the orders are 'in,' and not ' in front of,' Elbinger Alley. Perhaps it would even be the cleverest thing to do ; but the cleverest and the best are not always the same out here. No, we must go along it, for a hundred metres at least, because such are our orders, and then a hundred metres further because we mean to do the handsome thing. What they can do, we can do, even though they never probably had such ludicrously small forces at their disposal. But the uncanny horror of this scene, that might well overpower the soul, will have as strong an influence on them as on us. And it is just in these encounters by night that numbers count for less than the control a man has over himself. He is measured not against the enemy but against himself. So—take notice of nothing. To notice nothing is the least that can be done, and with this a man's self-respect begins to assert itself.

Once in a similar situation to this there were two men standing near each other. One of them suddenly looked at the other and said : ' Why, I believe you 're afraid.' The other answered : ' If you were half as afraid as I am you 'd have been somewhere else a long time since.'

There is no question which was the more courageous of the two. In danger there is nothing but the attitude a man has to himself. All else comes of itself.

When the ammunition has been handed over, the first part of our task is done. We arrange to keep in touch and, if the worst comes, to unite our forces at these cross-ways. A Verey light goes up. It comes from the enemy's block, but seems to rise from our feet. It falls sputtering on the top of the trench and colours the smoke, in which it dies out, with Bengal lights that fall with a red glow on the helmets of the men kneeling down close to one another. This gleam of helmet after helmet by night always has a calming effect. It makes an impression of silent, iron energy and of a gladiatorial impetus.

And now we must get to work. I have to space the men out at wide intervals, so that in case of a scrap each man will have full play. Then there will not be a panic and a crowding together at the first hold-up—a disaster past remedy by night in the confined space of the trenches. I have to choose out the most agile and daring fellows to go ahead as bombers ; but for the rear, too, there must be a trusty fellow to see that no one stays behind, and no one hangs back and that a chain of bombs is constantly passed on. The men of various arms have to be distributed along the line, the grenadiers who must shoot their rifle-grenades over the heads of the men in front so as to drop them on the enemy, the men with automatics and light machine-guns who can do no more in the dark than shoot straight up in the air. But as long as there is plenty of noise to distract the senses, every man believes for sure in the confusion that he and he alone is aimed at. I have to think, too, of the runners, the men with the bursting charges, the wire-cutters, the Verey-light pistols, the ammunition boxes, the haversacks full of bombs, and the pickaxes—for everything that may be wanted must be at hand. And after all there will be a load swapped here and there, a place changed. It is better to close an eye to this and allow men who like to stick together to do as they please, even though they put the order out ; for it is more important that the men should be suited together than the weapons they carry.

And when all this is done, one thing only remains for the officer in command. He must go the whole length of this chain of men whose hearts are beating with suspense and establish personal contact as the last essential. Each man must hear the sound of his officer's voice. What is said is all one, a word of cheer, a reminder, a question, a joke—it is not a matter of words that pass unheeded, but of the tone of the voice. Personal attention to every little detail now finds its reward, for it has a wonderful influence on a man to hear himself called by name at a moment when he himself has almost forgotten it. After this, the officer too takes his place, which, under all circumstances, is nearest the enemy.

We are now ready for work, a work long prepared for and on which much thought, industry, and strength of will have been expended. A destiny that neither we nor, indeed, any human agency could direct has set us down on this uncanny spot. In our childhood we never dreamed that such spots could possibly exist, and still less that we should find ourselves in them. But we, if any, are equal to such surroundings, and without a doubt we are equipped for our task ; and to be equipped, whatever the task and whatever the place, makes the man. Yesterday we were townsfolk, peasants, children, peaceable persons ; to-day we are fighters and our standards and our duties are different. To-day we have to kill and we shall kill without doubt —well and truly, without pity, and according to the rules of the art. We are scarcely more than fifty men as we stand at the entrance to this trench, but we have been through a dozen battles and tried for years in every form of war. We are no longer in possession of our first wild impetus, but in its place we have experience and coolness and this renders us no less formidable. This late, and perhaps last, phase of war is incorporated in a type of fighting man that is perfect of its kind ; it belongs to a clearly defined chapter of history and will for ever be part and parcel of the picture of the war. With a storm-troop composed of such men and armed with such weapons, one can match oneself with any opponent in the world. This is a feeling to fill one with pride and confidence.

And so forward ! The dark gateway receives us and we plunge into the shadow of the trench. It is so dark that we cannot see our hands before our eyes. The sergeant-major, whom I have to leave behind to hold his block, supports us by shooting a Verey light at brief intervals low over the trench in the direction we are going, so that we can take our bearings from time to time. We advance slowly, step by step, and every one is careful not to brush the side of the trench and to avoid the clatter of metal. Meanwhile the men holding the block help us, too, by trying to drown the sounds of our advance by incessant machine-gun fire. It is soon answered and followed as well by the dull explosion of bombs. We have scarcely started before a dead body blocks the trench. If this is the man sent out to get into touch, his fate soon overtook him. Immediately after, there is a strand or two of wire across the trench. H., who is second bomber, severs them carefully with his wire-cutters and doubles back the loose ends,

On again ! We come to a second dead body and then a low mound blocks the trench. Word to halt is passed from man to man, while an icy shudder traverses the spine. We smell a rat. Behind me I hear a panting breath. Two bombs in somebody's belt knock softly together. The further developments followed with a wild rapidity. Straight in front of us there was a muffled cry followed at once by a sharp metallic click. Then something is thrown and falls like a bit of wood on the mound and explodes almost at the same moment. At the same time there arises from both sides, as though from one compact body, a confused outcry. Verey lights rush up with a red glow on all sides and then unfold in light till we have a little sky of stars above us. We pull out the fuse cords of our bombs and throw them at a venture. At least a dozen unite in one reverberating explosion. The trench is shaken with the concussion and hidden in a cloud of snow-white smoke. A yellow rocket spirals up and then falls in rain of glowing stars, the signal probably for the English artillery whose thunder is now mingled with the tumult. In front of us and behind the machine-guns open out in a frenzy and wrap our ears in a cloak of deafening reports. Mingled with it are the rifle-grenades, whose discharge comes like a thump on our backs, and the grenades whistle like pound weights past our helmets. Sackfuls of bombs are passed along to the front and used up with in-conceivable speed. Bomb after bomb circles aloft into the silvery clouds of smoke and explodes in a blaze of fire.

Nothing can have survived in such a hailstorm of

fire. The cry goes up as though from one man—
Forward !   With a bound or two we are over the block,
and there lie two dead Englishmen surrounded by unused
bombs and their rifles thrown from them.   They died
but a moment ago.   The rigidity of death has not yet
gripped them and they lie as though they were asleep.
The sight of them inspires a savage joy and spurs us on.
It shows that we have only flesh and blood opposed to
us, and our mood is such that the devil could not stand
in our way.   On, then !

After this brutal outbreak of superior force, the
mopping-up of the trench proceeds with the methodical
and automatic precision of a trained storm-troop—a
precision speeded up to a pitch that only the rage of the
battle could maintain.   The trench is broken into a
zig-zag by frequent and massive traverses.   Between
every two there is a straight run of about eight metres.
The thing is to land a bomb in this space.   A single
one suffices ; for if the fragments of the bomb are not
fatal, the mere force of the explosion in this confined
space is so violent that nothing can withstand it.   Thus
the storming of the trench is punctuated by short
rushes.   There is a leap forward to duck behind the
massive block of the traverse, during which one throws
the bomb, hoping by judgment and guesswork to land
it in the trench further on ; and then there is another
rush forward almost simultaneously with the explosion
which long experience enables one to time to a second.
It is the mechanical co-operation of the man and his
missile, proceeding almost in silence and regulated only
by ejaculations, such as, ' Jump, throw, bombs forward, look out, heads down, now another, back, got

him ! ' Sometimes, two or three traverses further on, black balls are clearly seen high in the air against the white smoke. These have to be carefully marked so that they can be avoided by jumping like lightning forward or back. It is a game with life and death on the throw. It is no exaggeration to say that nothing more exciting can be imagined. For fear entirely vanishes. There is no time for it. Every fibre of the being is knit up in the two chances on which all there is is staked. The satisfaction of landing a well-aimed bomb, and the breathless suspense while one judges in the fraction of a second the flight of an enemy's bomb, make an interchange like light and darkness—but this mad chase of impressions flies past without pain, for you feel that your fate is in your own hands ; and this is quite another affair than being subjected passively to artillery fire for days on end. Then, too, it is we who set the pace here. This kind of fighting seems made for the German, with his feeling for discipline and order, analogous, one might say, to the musical co-ordination of an orchestra. As an old leader of shock-troops, I have rolled up many kilometres of trench in the teeth of all possible nations and I have always remarked the same thing. In this sort of fighting you never see your enemy, though never more than ten or twenty metres from him. At most you may catch sight of a shadow or two sneaking round a traverse ; and those you try to outreach at once with a bomb, so as either to cut off their retreat or to make them run back into the jaws of death. The English have only bombs with quick fuses, and hence they cannot, without very great risk to their lives, simply let them fall behind them to cover their retreat, and this is a very great advantage to us.   On the other hand, we have to wait a few seconds after pulling the fuse-cord before we throw, so that the explosion shall follow immediately the bomb pitches and thus allow the enemy no time to jump clear. Sometimes one explodes in the last stage of its flight. We call this a shrapnel throw.   It calls for coolness and command of one's weapon.

Behind nearly every traverse we come on a dead body with the blood oozing from numerous wounds caused by thin sharp splinters.   It is a brief glance only, for our eyes are more in the air than on the ground.   It is not a hard death : the force of the explosion takes life and consciousness away at once.   It is a strange feeling to leap forward over these dead whom you have never seen alive.   The satisfaction is a purely practical one, as though you saw before your eyes the expected result of an intelligent calculation and gave it a final assent. If it were oneself that was hit in such a moment, as I have been more than once, one would feel no more than the wonder of being so suddenly and incomprehensibly arrested, while the whole being was so bent on victorious activity that nothing else had any reality whatever.

Thus we go forward with a fierce elation, feeling that the force of the explosions that we send before us to clear the trench is our own.   Behind us, too, they are busy. Dull reverberations announce that bursting charges are being thrown down the dugout-shafts that we could not bother with, so that any living being that may have escaped may be annihilated.   Verey lights are shot off incessantly over our heads to light our way, and rifle-grenades are being fired to increase the range of our operations. Bombs pass without ceasing from hand to hand, and machine-guns are brought into action from behind the traverses and fired at a venture at the highest velocity. Now and then it happens that a man in the rear, overtaken by a sudden fury, appears among the leaders as they jump forward and back, and taking the foremost place deals with a few traverses on his own. One of them announces himself with ' Way for the Elders ' as though he were pushing his way through the bustle of some church ceremony. In these astonishing situations one always finds that men are far more astonishing still.

This wild career continues for a long time. Perhaps, too, it may be only some minutes, but they are so charged with action like a lightning dream that the sense of time loses all meaning. Then, again, in essentials, it is the same thing over and over again, and this produces a monotony of suspense which it is impossible to describe. It is like a continuous chain of duels, like a frightful game, or some very simple but dangerous sport. Finally we lose touch with the enemy after treading breathlessly on his heels all the while. This situation is more formidable than the fighting itself, during which we deprived them as they fled of the time required to organize their defence, and felt the superiority that gives the pursuer confidence and enthusiasm and ensures his success. No lights go up and a stillness succeeds in which for the first time we hear that the artillery is busy. The shells fall at a distance, for no one knows at headquarters who are masters of this stretch of trench. The reports on the other side must be as confused as on our own, and the situation cannot be put on the maps till to-morrow. They only know back there that infantry fighting is going on. We can hear, too, that we are not the only ones who have taken the enemy by the throat. From other parts of the battlefield as well comes the thin sharp rattle of machine-guns, mixed with the heavy detonations of bombs muffled by the narrow trenches. In front and behind is a loud outcry of wounded men, the familiar monotone on a piteous singing note, that stops and starts again at regular intervals.

We do not need to go much further forward before coming on a hastily constructed block, and here the game begins afresh. But now we have decidedly the worst of it. We are greeted with such a burst of bombs and rifle-grenades, that flame dances before our eyes and we have to make a hurried retreat. In the course of this the foremost throw themselves on those behind them and an indescribable panic ensues. Fortunately the enemy does not take full advantage of it ; other-wise he could make a massacre at his leisure of the tangled mob. Rifles are fired blindly, bombs with drawn fuses aimlessly chucked over the top, so that soil and flames spurt round our ears, a Verey light whizzes like a serpent of flame between our legs. Some attempt to climb on to the parapet and are dragged down by others who hang on to their legs or else fall back into the scrum.

At last the wave passes over to the rear. We come to our senses and have to consider now what is to be done next. The English, in spite of their haste, have selected a most advantageous position. Close behind their block can be seen the spoil of a trench that cuts

Elbinger Alley at right angles. Thus they are able to deploy rifle-grenade sections and machine-gunners on a wide front, the whole fire of which can be concentrated in front of their block. Hence we must at least withdraw beyond the range of a rifle-grenade, so that they cannot plaster us too heavily. Next I have two traverses knocked into the trench to make a block. By blocking thus the passage round the traverse, our front is at the least doubled. The two blocks are separated from each other by about thirty metres, and the second one is our real defence ; the object of the first is to compel the enemy to show himself for the space of a second lit up by the Verey lights. While holding the first block we pull down the wire entanglement from the parapet and fill the space between the two blocks with it. Next some bursting charges are fixed in the wire and their fuses attached by long cords that can be pulled from the second block. A narrow sap is then dug to a deep shell-hole near by, where a machine-gun is posted to give a little flanking fire. The rifle-grenadiers are distributed along the trench in recesses excavated in the walls and in front of the dugout entrances ; and then a desultory skirmish with rifle-grenades begins. As our Verey lights are getting scarce we have for the time to rely on the English in this respect ; the question of illumination is one of those that are disposed of by a species of tacit agreement. After this I send two men back to get into touch with the sergeant-major and to fetch a little bomb-thrower which we saw lying abandoned at the junction of Elbinger Alley and the hedge-trench. It will strengthen our hand, for it can throw a bomb weighing three pounds with fair accuracy to a distance of three hundred metres.

When all this has been done, it is time to consider the captured trench. We cannot leave the fire-steps unmanned, for example, further back ; for it is very possible that the trenches to our right and left are in the hands of the English. One side is not so dangerous, as there is a wire entanglement all along it. But the other is completely exposed, and a surprise attack from that direction would annihilate us. Then there are small trenches branching off to one side and the other. We disregard them in our first impetuosity, but now they must be blocked and held by posts. Uncertainty is the common feature of all situations of this kind. Danger surrounds us on every side.

The wounded, apart from the walking cases, are already collected in a large dugout. Most have been hit by fragments of bombs, and there are a few victims of one of our own bombs that went off in the stampede. It seems imperative to carry them back at least as far as Elbinger Alley as a start, for they are in considerable danger here, and any one who has been wounded himself knows how eager he is to be in safety once he can be of no further use. But stretcher-bearers must be sent from the rear, for we cannot spare a single man here. We are still in the thick of the fight.

We do not know what may happen with daylight, once the enemy realize our actual strength, and their reserves come streaming into the trenches. A report must be sent back immediately so that the night can be made full use of and measures taken. The artillery must have news of the alteration of the line, and the

R

large gaps between the isolated groups must be filled up by some means or other. Certainly it is a mystery how this is to be achieved. This strange way of fighting, by which the English eat slowly and methodically into our crumbling front, is in any case only possible with a large superiority of numbers and an ample power of initiative, and we can do little by isolated counter-attacks.

So I sit myself down in a large dugout still full of the suffocating fumes of a bursting charge, and scribble a report to battalion headquarters for Schmidt, who is wounded by a bomb splinter, to take back. There is nothing more I can do. We must await further developments. If the English, as may be expected, launch another extensive attack at dawn, we may perhaps be able to put up a defence, but we shall be easily cut off and surrounded. Then we may, according to circumstances, hold out for two or three days till the cooling water in the machine-guns has evaporated, till our ammunition is gone, and the trench is shot to blazes from every side by trench-mortars. This has happened a thousand times before. It is not a pleasant prospect ; but we must be prepared for it. When we used to read of sieges and holding out to the last man, we had quite another picture of it ; but in essentials it is always the same thing. The only difference is that it isn't so glorious, that not a cock will crow and not a single survivor perhaps carry the news of the last utmost exertions that will be expended before death finally hoists its standard over the churned and battered bit of trench. The thought of this causes a chilly feeling now and then.

For the time the best thing is to smoke a pipe by the light of a candle that Schüddekopf, who stuck to me like my shadow through it all, has planted in a niche. The tobacco is supplied me by the English who were passing their time together here before the bursting charges exploded among them. Their cap-badge is that of a colonial regiment, and a few yards further on are some dead of the Otago Regiment. It is clear from this that we have no chickens opposed to us. It would be good, too, to have a few hours' sleep, but this in spite of our terrible weariness is out of the question. Our nerves are overstrung and tremble like chords that have been struck with the hammer. Even when one has been for a long while in comfortable billets after a show, it is weeks before sleep recovers its full repose. The excitement that at the moment was too strong and too widely diffused to work itself out still has its reactions somewhere. Besides this, the spirit rises at such moments to a pitch of composure and clarity which is only to be accounted for by the reckless using up of one's reserve forces.

So there is nothing for it but to lie at length with a pipe in one's mouth and stare at the roof. A number of men lie round in the same way—just as they threw themselves down, waiting their turn to go on guard. Their coats about them, and their helmets on their heads, they lie motionless as though carved in wood. Only their eyes betray that they are living beings. This gloomy subterranean cavern makes a ghastly impression in the dim flicker of the candles. It seems as though the men lying there had stumbled in and fallen down beside each other after a large and consuming expression of life, after an unmeasured excess that drained them of their vital energies. The coma succeeding a debauch of death is ambushed in this narrow space from which time is excluded and where the resounding rattle of machine-guns penetrates as though into the recesses of a deep dream. The bodies lie with a leaden heaviness on the ground, and their thoughts that seem no longer to be part of them dart like silver fishes near the surface. The weight of fatigue is expressed in a feeling that one does not belong to it, and in a wonderful sense of taking everything for granted. What does one think about in such moments ? Actually one does not think at all, for the thoughts have an astonishingly alien quality. They seem to come from without and to play about the exhausted will like flies buzzing about a corpse. But the expression in the eyes will never be forgotten. They lie deep-sunken and staring above the prominent cheek-bones, and in them is reflected that unconscious thoughtfulness which is common to all extreme states of exhaustion, and seems to address its questioning direct to the great origin of things and to leave all their effects out of account.

Once more the racket outside swells to a sudden crisis and compels us to seize our arms and rush into the trench. With the first light of dawn an attempt has been made to force our block and has been beaten off. The white smoke of the bombs hovers still over the unoccupied stretch between the two blocks, and machine-gun fire sweeps it from both sides. The machine-gunners stand as though carved in stone behind their guns, and just behind the rampart of earth lies a man with his uniform torn with bomb splinters. It is the usual scene in trench block fighting. Sometimes it goes on unaltered for days except in the number of the dead, and this slowly increases.

And then an order from battalion headquarters comes along. It says that the front line is to be withdrawn to what was hitherto the support line and occupied by the reserve battalion. We can evacuate the Hedge-trench and retire to the embankment—there to be in reserve, though ready for an alarm. It is none too soon, for the first shells begin to fall near by.

The situation is now in hand all along our front, and the huge machine is set in motion for another day's work.

WE were not relieved before we had run our heads into the Copse once more. The attempt was made to surround it by rolling up the Sunk-road-trench without artillery preparation ; but the attempt was defeated. Then after a thorough preparation by the artillery we were put in in the Hedge-trench and Puisieux Alley. The aim was to make an encircling attack in co-operation with the divisional storm-troop. We had no luck with this enterprise either. A fully loaded lorry was wiped out by a direct hit as it was coming into Achiet. In Puisieux Alley the leading section was held up by bursting charges, and we others in the hedge-trench first had heavy losses from our own artillery and then, just as we were rolling it up, a company of New Zealanders appeared as though by magic on our flank. We were shot down and dealt with by bombs, and there were very few survivors of the slaughter. After this we were kept for two days in an unfamiliar bit of trench, where at last the dead outnumbered the living, before we were finally relieved by detachments of the 164th Regiment. There is no space for a detailed description of all this, and in any case it would only be an endless repetition. Even now one event can scarcely be disentangled from another in my memory.

Now, however, we have really been taken out. In Achiet, where we detrained when we first arrived on this front, the lorries are waiting and soon we are embarked again on the same journey through the desolate battlefields, past devastated villages and lonely trench crossings. The future is uncertain, for we know from experience that to be in reserve only means that more fighting is before us. And the stronger the group whose reserves we join the shorter our rest will be, for the wider the front the more numerous are its critical spots. Also times are far from restful, as we can hear from the thunder of the offensive developing in our rear.

Once back there, where the gun-flashes quiver incessantly, we take leave of Copse 125, whose last remains are now being pounded by our own artillery. The events of the few weeks we spent there will soon fade in the impressions of new and sanguinary experiences that succeed each other at ever shorter intervals like nightmare visions.

To be sure, nothing of importance happened there, compared with the great events of these days ; but for us personally it was important all the same. We even lost it, but we cannot be reproached for that. All that could have been done we did. It was done first and last out of simple feelings without the assistance of any sublime point of view. It was done in the spirit of sheer self-sacrifice, and on that scene we stood for our country not in word but in deed. For if we have learned anything at all out here it is that deeds are above all else. We shall carry that on with us into the years of peace ; for though times of sanguinary conflict are rare, a man must always give himself up heart and soul to that in which he believes.

Shell-hole and trench have a limited horizon. The

range of vision extends no further than a bomb-throw; but what is seen is seen very distinctly. The fighter stands up against the fearful monotony of this background as a figure of tragic intensity, and in these moments when death rises up in flame a man is seen for what he is. Once more we have been able here to see and to feel that a German is a match for any fate. We have learnt to believe in him and to rely on him for the utmost. And when one looks at these men who are borne in silence, helmet by helmet, to the song of the engine towards fresh ordeals—this new and iron race tempered in every fibre—one can only wish that the country may not lose them all. This breed must not pass away like a meteor, quenched in darkness after a blaze of splendour never seen before. Its men have shown in this war that there is nothing that cannot be done for an ideal, and it is they who must perpetuate the memory and drive home the consequences of their deeds. They are changed men within, and this will find its expression in every sphere of life.

Copse 125 that sinks below the horizon at our backs in thunder and flame leaves its traces in the hearts of the survivors. More than is dreamed of to-day took place on that fiery island.